THE FATE OF ADELAIDE

L.E.L., by Maclise

The Fate of Adelaide,
A Swiss Romantic Tale;
and Other Poems

by

Letitia Elizabeth Landon

"L.E.L."

A FACSIMILE REPRODUCTION
WITH AN INTRODUCTION AND INDEXES
EDITED BY F. J. SYPHER

SCHOLARS' FACSIMILES & REPRINTS
DELMAR, NEW YORK
1990

SCHOLARS' FACSIMILES & REPRINTS
ISSN 0161-2279
SERIES ESTABLISHED 1936
VOLUME 447

Published by Scholars' Facsimiles & Reprints
Delmar, New York 12054-0344, U.S.A.

New matter in this edition
© 1990 Academic Resources Corporation
All rights reserved

Printed and made in the United States of America

REPRODUCED FROM A COPY IN
AND WITH THE PERMISSION OF
THE BRITISH LIBRARY

Library of Congress Cataloging-in-Publication Data

L. E. L. (Letitia Elizabeth Landon), 1802-1838.

The fate of Adelaide, a Swiss romantic tale, and other poems /
by Letitia Elizabeth Landon ("L.E.L.") ;
with an introduction and indexes edited by F. J. Sypher
    p.   cm. –
(Scholars' Facsimiles & Reprints, ISSN 0-0161-7729 ; v. 447)
"Reproduced from a copy in . . . the British Library"
–T.p. verso.
Originally published: London : J. Warren, 1821.
Includes bibliographical references (p.   ) and index.
    ISBN 0-8201-1447-2
    I. Sypher, F. J. II. Title.
III. Series: Scholars' Facsimiles & Reprints (Series) ; v. 447.
    PR4865.L5F38   1990
   821'.7–dc20   90-8961
                    CIP

Contents

Introduction, 7
Title-page of *The Fate of Adelaide*, 1821, [i]
To Mrs. Siddons, [iii]
Preface, [v]
The Fate of Adelaide, Canto I., 1
———, Canto II., 31
Miscellaneous Poems, 67
The Farewell, 69
Lines to ———, 71
Fragment, 73
Absence, 75
Curtius, 77
Sketch of a Painting of Santa Malvidera, escaped miraculously from Shipwreck, 81
Sonnet, 83
Sonnet, 84
Stanzas, 85
The Village of the Lepers, 86
Lines on ———, 88
Fragment, 91
Portrait, 93
To ———, 95
Corinna, 97
Sleeping Child, 99
Lines Addressed to Colonel H———, on his return from Waterloo, 101
Love's Parting Wreath, 103
Answer, 105
Dirge, 107
Sonnet, 109
Absence, 110
A Lover's Dream, 113
The Phoenix and the Dove, 115
Love's Choice, 116
The Star, 117

CONTENTS

Stanzas, Adapted to Music by ——, 119
Answer to ——, 121
Castle Building, 123
Fable, 125
Sketch of Scenery, 129
Lines to ——, 133
Lines Addressed to Miss Bisset, 135
Fragment, 137
Lines, 139
The Storm, 141
To Sir John Doyle, Bart., 146
Fragment, 149
Addressed to ——, 154

Index of titles, 157

Index of first lines, 159

Illustrations

frontispiece
L.E.L., by Maclise

following page 34
22 Hans Place
45 Brompton Row
William Jerdan, by Maclise
Mrs. Siddons, by Downman

Introduction

Of Letitia Elizabeth Landon it might almost be said, as Byron remarked of himself, that she "awoke one morning" and found herself "famous." It is surprising to recall the flowering of her fame during the reigns of George IV (1820-1830) and of William IV, "the sailor king" (1830-1837), when Shelley and Keats were scorned or unknown, Dickens and Thackeray, Carlyle and Mill were just beginning their careers, and Ruskin and Arnold were children. Scott, Moore, and Byron reigned in poetry; in fiction, Scott again (but under a cloak of anonymity, as "The Author of *Waverly*"), followed by younger writers like Bulwer and Disraeli. In the nations of Europe, as in England, reaction and revolution ebbed and flowed as society wrestled with the consequences of rapid industrialization and urbanization, and the correlative acquisition and management of colonial empires.

Into this scene, almost by accident, stepped a teenager who went on to become one of the most admired English poets of her time, and whose eclipse, after her tragic death in Africa at the age of thirty-six, was almost as sudden as her emergence. The full history of her reputation is too complex to be told here, since it involves nothing less than the vast social and cultural transformations of the era named after the longest-reigning monarch in British history, Queen Victoria. But in the space available it is possible to give some indications of how the "star" named "L.E.L." was born.

Her father, John Landon (1756-1824), was the eldest son of Elizabeth and the Reverend John Landon (1722-1782; son of Thomas Landon, of Credenhill, Herefordshire), rector (1749-1782) of the small rural parish of Tedstone Delamere, in Herefordshire. There is a tradition of connection with "Sir William Landon, Knt." of Crednall but I have been unable to find verification of this. However, record exists of a commoner named William Landon, of Crednall (apparently an alternate spelling of "Credenhill"), Herefordshire, who was the father of John Landon (1700-1777), rector (1754-1761) of Nurstead with Ifield, Kent, author of tracts, who died at Tedstone Court, Herefordshire, and to whom there is a memorial tablet at the church at Tedstone Delamere.[1] The families are undoubtedly related,

INTRODUCTION

but to clarify the relationships is beyond the scope of this inquiry. There are, in any case, numerous records of persons named Landon in Herefordshire; also, several emigrants of the name left Herefordshire and settled in colonial Massachusetts.[2]

John Landon—unlike his father, and his brothers, Whittington (1758-1838), and James (1764-1850), who made their careers in the Church—entered the navy as a midshipman,[3] possibly about the time of the American Revolution; he made two voyages (by which one should probably understand absences of several years in each case), one to the south coast of Africa, and one to Jamaica. His naval career is said to have depended on the patronage of his friend and relative, Admiral Sir George Bowyer (b. ca. 1740), around the time of whose retirement from active service in 1794, and death in 1800,[4] John Landon left the navy and obtained a job as a "superior clerk" in Mr. Adair's army agency, 25 Pall Mall, which during the French wars (1793-1815) was a profitable business, yielding thousands of pounds a year.[5] Adair eventually retired and sold the business to three of his associates, one of whom was the poet's father, whose experience and family connections in the military must have been a valuable asset to the firm.

About this same time, John Landon married Catherine Jane Bishop (d. 1854), who is said to have brought £14,000 to their match.[6] The bride's mother, Mrs. Bishop (d. ca. 1826), a woman of independent income, became in later years very close to her granddaughter, who lived with her in Sloane Street for a time, and looked after her with patience and devotion. Her family name may have been Cahet (see L.E.L.'s letter of 1820 to her mother, quoted below; but this improbable spelling looks as if it could be a misprint or a misreading of the MS. for Cabet or Cabot).

On 14 August 1802, Letitia Elizabeth Landon was born at 25 Hans Place, Chelsea, a neighborhood where she was destined to spend most of her adult life. Hans Place, Sloane Street, and adjacent areas were a quiet residential quarter, then almost in the suburbs, but soon to be engulfed by the rapidly growing city of London. "Hans Town," as the neighborhood was at first called, had been planned and built around 1780 by Henry Holland (1745-1806), and named after Sir Hans Sloane (1660-1753), a prominent physician who had purchased the manor of Chelsea in 1712. The houses were attractively plain, brick structures, designed in typical Georgian style, intended to be rented to upper middle class and professional people.[7]

The Landons' house, with its rose gardens, had once been lived in by the architect's son, Captain Holland; it stood at the southwest corner of the enclosed square of Hans Place, across the street from No. 22, where L.E.L. attended school, and in later years resided. In the distance, at this early date, lay the open field of Chelsea common, with detached houses on its circumference. Close by was "Sloane Place," the show-piece mansion that Holland built as his own residence, with its beautiful trees and gardens, including a small lake with a little island in it. This may have been a favorite scene of the poet's early childhood, and a model for the Crusoe-like island kingdom that she made her own later on, when she was living in the country. The island is a recurrent image in her writing, where it is a symbol of the world of the imagination and of art and song and love, a refuge from the ills and stresses of the "actual" world, as in the following lyric, perfect in its harmonious combination of delight and regret, ecstasy and elegy:[8]

Song.

As steals the dew upon the flower
So stole my love on thee
I cannot tell the day nor hour
I first loved thee!

But now in every scene and clime
In change of grief or glee,
I only measure from the time
I first saw thee.

I only think while fast and fair
My good ship cuts the sea,
I leave the lovely island where
I first loved thee.

The wide world has one only spot
Where I would wish to be,
Where all the rest of life forgot
I first loved thee!

At the age of five, Letitia began attending Miss Rowden's school at 22 Hans Place. Far from being a superficial finishing-school for girls, this was a serious educational establishment, quite remarkable

INTRODUCTION

in its time.[9] The school had its roots in the Abbey School at Reading, where Jane Austen had been a pupil. At a later date Monsieur Dominique de Saint Quentin, a refugee from the French Revolution, who had formerly been secretary to the last French ambassador to the Court of St. James's under Louis XVI, joined the staff as an extremely successful teacher of French (and other subjects), and author of textbooks. He soon married the English teacher there, who was a partner of the proprietor, on whose retirement the Saint Quentins took over the school and moved it to London in the summer of 1798; Monsieur de Saint Quentin continued to teach, but Madame devoted herself to administrative duties. There Lady Caroline Lamb was a pupil for a period (ca. 1798)—brief and apparently difficult for all parties.[10] And there Mary Russell Mitford was sent (1798-1802) by her parents, who had befriended Monsieur de Saint Quentin in Reading. The English teacher in London, Frances Arabella Rowden, who had formerly been a respected governess in the Bessborough family, became her special tutor outside of school, often taking her to the theater, both in her years as a boarder and during visits later on.

At the time of Letitia's attendance, Monsieur de Saint Quentin was evidently still teaching French, since she is said to have been fortunate in acquiring an elegant French accent from him. And she began her acquaintance with the classics of English literature there, memorization and recitation of set pieces being a prominent part of the program—no doubt partly a result of Miss Rowden's enthusiasm for the drama. She was herself a poet, the author of two modestly successful volumes of verse: *A Poetical Introduction to the Study of Botany* (1801; three editions); and *The Pleasures of Friendship* (1810; three editions)—and of a book on mythology (1820) and one on authors (1821). She is described as "full of energy, kind, devoted to what she esteemed the highest of all professions, that of education."[11] On the retirement of the Saint Quentins, Miss Rowden headed the school, and in the early 1820s moved it to Paris, where she married the Comte de Saint Quentin, now a widower, who had inherited his title and his marriageability. The story of the school offers ample room for reflection and imaginative reconstruction. In any case it is apparent that Letitia, the young poet-to-be, was in a stimulating environment during her two years there.

During this prosperous time her father took a financial interest in "Coventry Farm," which consisted of 127 acres in the county of Middlesex, between Highwood Hill and Edgware (where the

INTRODUCTION

Coventry family had been long established). His investments were apparently based on a leasehold, since the property was owned (until 1866) by descendants of William Lee, who had bought it from the Coventry family in 1762.[12] A brother of John Landon's seems to have been in charge of the daily operations, while the poet's father divided his attention between his work as an army agent in London, and their experiments in model farming. Agriculture was then an exciting and promising science, as much in the throes of revolution as manufacturing was, and during the war years prices of farm produce were high and arable areas were increased. Costly expenditures must have been made by the Landons in such things as modern farming machinery and farm buildings, perhaps also special types of seed or breeds of livestock. Memoirists of L.E.L. tend to censure her father's extravagance in this venture, and his brother's poor management; but John Landon surely realized that the war would eventually end, and that the profits of the army agency would decline, so it would in the meantime be desirable to spare no expense in developing some other source of livelihood for the future of his family and for his retirement (he being about fifty years old at this time). Also, his early years in Herefordshire must have instilled in him a love of rural life and agricultural pursuits.

It was undoubtedly with the motive of devoting greater attention to Coventry Farm that shortly after Letitia's seventh birthday, in 1809, John Landon moved with his family to East Barnet, Hertfordshire (about five miles due east of the farm), where his brother had taken a lease on a large, gabled, somewhat dilapidated but handsome country house dating from the early seventeenth century, and known, with its surrounding gardens and more than 48 acres of grounds, as "Trevor Park" after Thomas Trevor (1658-1730), who had acquired it ca. 1690.[13] The house, originally called "Church Hill House," after its location, had been built by Thomas Conyers (d. 1615), and was remembered as the place where in 1611 Lady Arabella Stuart (1575-1615; cousin of King James I, and next after him in line of succession to Queen Elizabeth) was held prisoner and escaped disguised as a man. She had been secretly married to William Seymour against the king's will, and when word got out she was arrested. Her plan was to meet Seymour in London and thence flee to France, but the meeting did not take place and before reaching Calais she was taken prisoner again, to spend the brief remainder of her life in the Tower of London.[14] The old house at Trevor Park, grand but decayed, with its romantic but unhappy story, must have made a vivid impression on

INTRODUCTION

L.E.L. and she later drew on her memories of the house in writing the descriptions of old country houses that appear in her novels.

The environment of Trevor Park was also an important stimulus to her poetic imagination at a time when her gifts were rapidly developing. There were few other children in the neighborhood, and although her younger brother, Whittington (b. 23 June 1804)[15] was her playmate and companion, much of her free time seems to have been spent alone—reading books from the well-stocked library at the house, and wandering in the old half-overgrown gardens and in the nearby fields and woods. She herself wrote: "I cannot remember the time when composition in some shape or other was not a habit. I used to invent long stories, which I was only too glad if I could get my mother to hear. These soon took a metrical form; and I used to walk about the grounds, and lie awake half the night, reciting my verses aloud."[16]

Her education was supervised by a cousin of hers, Elizabeth Landon, who recalled her pupil's "extraordinary memory and genius" not only in mastery of her studies but also in her creative faculties.[17] Her cousin's character and interests and choice of books must have played an important role too; one would like to know more about her, but she insists on remaining in the background. L.E.L. mentions reading a life of Petrarch,[18] "which perhaps first threw round Italy that ideal charm it has always retained in my eyes"; the *Odyssey*; and of course, Scott, whom she calls the "greatest influence in forming my style."[19] She is said (perhaps with pardonable exaggeration) to have known "the whole"[20] of *The Lady of the Lake* (1810) by heart (approximately 5,000 lines!); she must have loved the idea of the island in the lake. Scott's poems are presently out of fashion, but it is worth recalling that they created a sensation at the time, and for at least a hundred years afterwards they were read, enjoyed, and admired by nearly everyone.

A book not directly mentioned by L.E.L. but which certainly had a profound influence on her is Madame de Staël's *Corinne ou l'Italie* (1807; two different English versions appeared the same year), with its glorious scene of Corinne's coronation as poet laureate in Rome (cf. the poem "Corinna," p. 97 of this reprint), and its moving story of love growing and deepening amid the artistic splendors of Italy. The figure of Corinne, who lives an independent life as a poet, served as a role-model for countless women, who read her book as they toured Italy, and aspired to a life like hers. The book that made L.E.L. famous, *The Improvisatrice*, echoes *Corinne*, and L.E.L. later

INTRODUCTION

translated Corinne's French improvisations into English poems that appeared in the much-reprinted translation of the novel (1833), by Isabel Hill (1800-1842).

Others among L.E.L.'s favorite books at this time were *Robinson Crusoe*, the *Arabian Nights*, the *Voyages* of Captain Cook, and a children's book, *The Travels of Sylvester Tramper through the Interior of South Africa*, by George Walker (London, 1813).[21] In this reading one senses the influence of her father, who not only gave her some of the books, but also must have told her stories of his own adventures in the navy, especially in Africa. Similarly, the knowledge and love of the stars and of trees and flowers that runs through L.E.L.'s writings must reflect her sharing in her father's experience at sea and in the English countryside.

Her attachment to her father was all the stronger because of a certain coolness that prevailed between her and her mother, especially after the birth of her much younger sister, about 1812. The child was weak in health and only lived for about thirteen years, requiring her mother's constant attention. About the same time, her brother was sent away to the Merchant Taylors' School in London, so one can well sympathize with the elder daughter's eagerness in going to wait at the gate in the evening for her father to come home, as she describes it in her autobiographical story, "The History of a Child," in *Traits and Trials of Early Life* (London, 1836). William Jerdan, who knew the family well, describes John Landon as a man of "simple heartedness, kindly nature, and quiet worth."[22] His daughter's devotion is crystallized in the moving elegiac lines at the conclusion of "The Troubadour."

L.E.L.'s first formal literary work was a no longer extant composition on the American adventures of a cousin of hers, Captain Landon (possibly in the War of 1812). She also wrote a "sketch" (see pp. 146-48 of the reprinted text) of General Sir John Doyle (1750-1834), a hero of the Peninsular War, whom she later knew as the great-uncle of her friend Rosina Doyle Wheeler, who married Edward Bulwer. The military connections and sympathies formed under her father's influence and family connections remained a constant in L.E.L.'s life, even down to her last residence in England, at the home of her friends and relatives, General and Mrs. Fagan, and her marriage in 1838 to George Maclean (1801-1847), who held the rank of captain in the British army.

The victory at Waterloo in 1815 secured relief from war, but peace brought its own unhappy consequences.[23] Naturally there was a

INTRODUCTION

sudden drop in the demand for military supplies, including foodstuffs; but when England tried to export her produce and manufactures to Europe, it soon became apparent that the economies of the European nations had been so devastated that they could offer no market. The price of grain fell dramatically, and political unrest grew amid nationwide depression, as thousands became unemployed. John Landon's fortunes had depended on the one hand upon the war industry, and on the other upon agriculture. The turn of events thus fell doubly hard on him, and consequently the family in 1815 had to give up their residence at Trevor Park. The proprietor, Mrs. Smith, reoccupied the house, and shortly after her death in 1818, it was torn down and the gardens ploughed up for use as farmland. Even the brook had its course altered. For L.E.L. it seemed as if her whole world had been demolished, and throughout her writings a morbid fascination with ruin and destruction, and with unrecoverable dreams of the past echoes the deep emotional trauma of this uprooting.

As one reads her fiction and poetry, one also has the impression that L.E.L. during the years at Trevor Park had formed a romantic attachment which was severed, perhaps at first by her family's departure, and finally by the eventual marriage of the other party. This is mere conjecture from her works, and there is no external indication of such an episode, although it is hardly unimaginable that something of the sort might have occurred. In any case the theme of youthful love and separation is recurrent in her writings, along with the theme of destruction of beautiful and beloved places, and both of these seem to be based upon the intensely felt experience of her own early years.

After their departure from Trevor Park, the Landons lived at Lewis Place, Fulham, for a year, and in 1816 moved to 45 Brompton Row. Adair & Co. had been dissolved, and they lived in relatively straitened circumstances and, in L.E.L.'s own words, "great seclusion";[24] but nevertheless as tenants of a handsome mansion, surrounded by gardens, in what was then an almost rural, certainly suburban part of London. During this period of retrenchment, the Landons considered "a thousand projects" for the improvement of their material position, and in an age of best-sellers, when writers like Scott and Byron had made fortunes almost overnight, the potential value of their daughter's prodigious literary talent was taken into calculated account.

As it happened, the Landons' next-door neighbor in Brompton was William Jerdan (1782-1869), editor of a recently established but

INTRODUCTION

already influential weekly journal, *The Literary Gazette* (begun 25 January 1817). Jerdan's account of his first impression of L.E.L. is unforgettable:

> My cottage overlooked the mansion and grounds of Mr. Landon, the father of L.E.L., at Old Brompton; a narrow lane only dividing our residences. My first recollection of the future poetess is that of a plump girl, grown enough to be almost mistaken for a woman, bowling a hoop round the walks, with the hoop-stick in one hand and a book in the other, reading as she ran, and as well as she could manage both exercise and instruction at the same time. The exercise was prescribed and insisted upon: the book was her own irrepressible choice.[25]

She would have been fourteen or more at that time, and her reading must have been in large part an expression of rebellion against the exercise, which seems childish for someone her age, and probably was "prescribed" because they wanted her to keep her weight down and because they thought it unhealthy for her to spend so much time immersed in reading and writing. One could say she was compelled to illustrate in person the proverbial saying–she who runs may read.

Letitia's mother mentioned to their literary neighbor that her daughter was "addicted" to "poetical composition" and asked if he would be willing to "peruse a few of her efforts." The word "addicted" is significant—one imagines that reading and writing now all the more built that island of fantasy where her spirit sought refuge from the unhappy cloud that had descended upon her family, who, for their part, undoubtedly recognized that there was something feverish about their daughter's literary activity. The poet's cousin and tutor forwarded some poems to Jerdan with a polite, deferential covering letter dated 13 February 1820. He returned them the following day; they were rewritten and resubmitted with other pieces.[26] Jerdan was impressed, but could not believe that Letitia, whom he had seen playing with his own children, could be the author. He suspected that Elizabeth had actually written the poems, and was concealing her authorship under cover of her pupil, so he challenged Letitia to a test. One day, while they were driving back to Brompton from town, as they passed St. George's Hospital, Hyde Park Corner, it was suggested that Letitia write a poem on it when they got home. They arrived, dined, and by tea-time, an hour later, the author had produced, to Jerdan's astonishment, a seventy-four line poem

INTRODUCTION

(published in *The Improvisatrice*, 1824) in hardly more time than would have been adequate for the inscription on paper of a fair copy.[27]

On Saturday, 11 March 1820, in No. 164 of *The Literary Gazette*, appeared her first publication, a poem titled "Rome," signed simply "L." The text is worth quoting, partly because of its firstness and partly because of its expression of one of the recurrent themes of her poetry, the "vanity of human wishes." The style is somewhat declamatory, more like Hemans than the later Landon, but it has a seriousness and a vividness that prefigure her mature writing (in spite of the "utter mistake"–Jerdan's words–in the fourth line):

ROME.

Oh! how thou art changed, thou proud daughter of fame,
Since that hour of ripe glory, when empire was thine,
When earth's purple rulers, kings, quailed at thy name,
And thy capitol worshipped as Liberty's shrine.

In the day of thy pride, when thy crest was untamed,
And the red star of conquest was bright on thy path,
When the meteor of death thy stern falchion's edge flamed,
And earth trembled when burst the dark storm of thy wrath.

But Rome thou art fallen! the memory of yore,
Only serves to reproach thee with what thou art now:
The joy of thy triumph for ever is o'er,
And sorrow and shame set their seal on thy brow.

Like the wind shaken reed, thy degenerate race,
The children of those once the brave and the free–
Ah, who can the page of thy history trace,
Nor blush, thou lost city, blush deeply for thee!

Could the graves yield their dead, and thy warriors arise,
And see thy blades rusted, thy war banners furl'd,
Would they know the proud eagle that soared thro' the skies,
Whose glance lightened over a terror struck world?

Yet e'en in disgrace, in thy sadness and gloom,
An halo of splendour is over thee cast:

INTRODUCTION

It is but the death-light that reddens the tomb,
And calls to remembrance the glories long past.

This was followed in the next issue (18 March) by a sweet lyric, "The Michaelmas Daisy"—an echo of Moore's "The Last Rose of Summer." Two further poems were published in August, and in October a poem titled "Vaucluse" (alluding to Petrarch), with some additional, untitled lines, and a sonnet in November.[28]

By this time an ambitious plan to publish a book of Letitia's poetry was well in hand. She and her grandmother had left around August for a four-month-long visit with relatives at Clifton (famous for the picturesque, though not Alpine beauty of the Avon gorge) and at "Castle-end," Gloucestershire. From there, she sent back the "first canto" of *The Fate of Adelaide* for Jerdan to look over:[29]

Dear Sir,

    Having now rendered my first canto as perfect as is in my power, I now venture to intrude it on your notice. I am too well aware of my many defects, and the high advantages of your opinion, not to anxiously avail myself of your permission to submit it to your inspection. Of the poem itself I have nothing more to say than that your judgment will be most unmurmuringly and implicitly relied on. It is quite at your option to throw it behind the fire, or allow it a little longer existence.

    But however delightful your praise may be, is it presumption to say, do not let me receive from your kindness what I would owe to your real sentiments?

    Before I conclude, I must be permitted to express my pleasure on seeing I had been honoured with a place in the "Gazette." Pray accept my best thanks for the improvements you made.

                    Believe me, dear Sir,
                      Ever yours most gratefully,
                      Letitia Elizabeth Landon.

This letter was probably written after the appearance of "Vaucluse" in *The Literary Gazette* on Saturday, 21 October, and both the letter and the poem were sent to her mother, who forwarded them to Jerdan with the following covering letter with its allusion to the pecuniary motives for publishing the book:

INTRODUCTION

Wednesday, Nov. 4th.

My dear Sir,

 Again I am intruding upon your time, having received the enclosed from Letitia. Your former kindness induces my taking the liberty of asking you to look them over. Need I say how very anxious she is for your opinion? I trust you will not think her arrogant, as I believe you are aware of her reasons for wishing to publish. I shall send to her next week. Perhaps you will do her the favour of then giving her your opinion. Need I say how very anxious she is to learn her fiat.

In very great haste,
Most truly yours,
C. J. Landon.

 Jerdan's encouraging response can be inferred from the letter that Letitia wrote to her cousin Elizabeth at this time:[30]

Dear Cousin,

 Are you pleased with me? Am I not happy? "An elegance of mind peculiarly graceful in a female";—is not this the praise you would have wished me to obtain? Has all your trouble been thrown away? It has always been my most earnest wish to do something that might prove your time had not been altogether lost. To excel is to show my grateful affection to you. The poem is now entirely finished. I hope you will like "Adelaide." I wished to pourtray a gentle soft character, and to paint in her the most delicate love. I fear her dying of it is a little romantic; yet, what was I to do, as her death must terminate it? Pray do you think, as you are the model of my, I hope, charming heroine, you could have contrived to descend to the grave

"Pale martyr to love's wasting flame?"

Not only is the second canto concluded, but I have written all the minor pieces I intend inserting. And now, dear cousin, I do so long to be with you, if it were only to show you how amiable I intend being. I will not be passionate; and, as to Elizabeth, I will

be so good-natured—I will be to her what you have been to me. . .
. . I never knew how delightful it was to be at home until I was
away. It is all very pleasant to go out for a day or two. I do not
mean to say I do not like it, but when it comes to be week upon
week and month upon month (for it is now four months since I
saw any of you) I am heartily tired. . . . . I hate to be continually
obliged to think of what I must say, for fear of offending some
one or other—however, I never had the slightest disagreement
with one of them. On the whole, I compare my visit to Clifton to
a sunny day in December. . . . . I have such a delightful room to
sit in, where I usually spend mornings and evenings—I have
borrowed Miss Elizabeth Smith's "Fragments," I like them so
much. I am quite in Miss C.'s good graces—it is impossible to help
laughing at her, but it never offends her—on the contrary she
exclaims, "Well now, dear heart alive, I am so glad to find you
have such good spirits!" I believe my aunt thinks me not a little
rhodomontade, but it is very excusable at present. I am happy for
three things; first, I am so enchanted with Mr. Jerdan's note;
secondly, so pleased at having left Clifton; and last, though not
least, I am so delighted to think it will not be long before I shall
see you all again.

The youthful enthusiasm of the writer's reaction to Jerdan's
words of praise is as contagious as it must have been annoying to her
hosts—having such a self-satisfied guest, who seems to have been
unable to resist making fun of one of the household, who in turn
sounds remarkably good-natured. It is hard for a modern reader to
know how to gauge Jerdan's phrase "particularly graceful in a
female"; it sounds condescending, but it was evidently taken as a high
compliment. Certainly, Jerdan sincerely admired and respected her
poetic abilities—perhaps one can infer that he meant "elegance of
mind" of a kind both admirable and distinctively womanly—an
interpretation which accords with early nineteenth-century notions of
women and men as possessing distinct qualities of intellect and spirit.
The reference to "Elizabeth" obviously does not refer to her cousin,
to whom she is addressing the letter, and seems therefore as if it may
refer to her sister, then about eight years old, to whom (this seems to
imply) Letitia was in the habit of being ill-natured, rather than good-
natured; she also implies that she often responded to her cousin with
outbursts of temper ("I will not be passionate"). The *Fragments in
Prose and Verse* (1808) of the oriental scholar and translator,

INTRODUCTION

Elizabeth Smith (1776-1806) were frequently reprinted (see *DNB*).

At about the same time as this letter, perhaps even with the same post, she wrote to her mother as follows:

> At present, all I have to say is, that I do so long to see you all, that I like my aunt more and more, that nothing can be pleasanter than my visit to Castle-end, and that I only wish you were in as agreeable a place. I have but one cause of complaint—I so seldom hear from any of you. As for my cousin, if I did not know her too well, I should take it for granted she had forgotten me. You cannot think how delightful a letter is—it makes me quite happy for three days. The following lines I wrote last night I send them, as they are addressed to you.
>
> > "I will not say, I fear your absent one
> > Will be forgotten, but you cannot feel
> > The sickening thoughts that o'er the spirit steal
> > When I remember I am quite alone.
> > That all I loved most fondly, all are gone.
> > To you that deepest sorrow is unknown;
> > Some very dear ones are beside you now;
> > But cold to me each smile that meets my own;
> > It does not beam upon some long-loved brow.
> > 'Tis vain to tell me we again shall meet,
> > That thought but makes the weary hours depart
> > More slowly; hope is tedious to the heart
> > When we so oft its accents must repeat.
> > Absence is to affection, as the hour
> > Of winter's chilling blight upon the spring's young flower."
>
> I have now, entirely lost my former passion for travelling. If I am so tired of what can scarcely be called a long journey, what should I do in my intended travels through Africa! I have not written to you since you enclosed Mr. Jerdan's note. How happy I am! it so far surpasses my expectations, convinced as I am that a kind of curse hangs over us all; it seemed too delightful to happen to one of the Cahets.... To say the truth, I had thought so much about the poem, that I had got quite tired of it, and at last sent it in a fit of despair. So favourable a verdict again revived the spirit of exertion. I had, indeed, compounded a miserable essence for expectation—it might have been styled

INTRODUCTION

intrusion, presumption, or, to sum up in a word, it might have been good for nothing. The poem I took with me to Clifton, intending to finish it, I quarrelled with and burnt. This one has been entirely written since I was there, and is now completely terminated.—"My task is ended now." . . . . I have made your purse scarlet. I think, though, they say green is the colour of hope; it has been an unlucky colour to us, for how fond we all were of it! . . . My aunt is really a delightful person—so good-natured, lets me do just as I please; I dont wonder they all like her so much. When do you *think* of moving? Once together again, and I care not for anything. . . . I think you will smile when I tell you I often spend an evening engaged in a sober rubber at whist.

She is eighteen years old as she writes, but much of this sounds like the voice one hears all through her writing; as in, for example, her fear of being forgotten, and the extreme loneliness that came on her at night, when she composed the lines to her mother (included in this collection, p. 75). The reference to her "intended travels through Africa" naturally leaps to one's eyes as a reminder of long-nurtured childhood dreams that encouraged her attraction to the man she married in 1838. And the sense of a "kind of curse" hanging over the whole family illustrates the constant feeling of foreboding and fated early death that runs throughout her writing. The allusion to the color green must refer to Trevor Park and Coventry Farm. Her definition of a delightful person being one who lets her do just as she pleases is witty, but also revealing of the independent spirit that was destined to bring her to such grief in later years, when she was in the spotlight before a jealous censorious society that did not at all want to let her do just as she pleased. Indeed, taking this and the previous letter together, one can clearly see the outlines of her character—her talent and conscientious determination, with her need for praise and encouragement; her wit and independence, with her need to love and be loved; her tendencies to playfulness, mockery, anger, nostalgia, and depression.

One infers that with this letter to her mother, L.E.L. enclosed, for Jerdan's approval, the "Second Canto" and the "minor pieces" that were to complete the volume. Catherine Landon forwarded them to Jerdan with the following covering letter, apparently written from the address of her mother, Mrs. Bishop:

INTRODUCTION

138, Sloane-street, Nov. 27th.

My dear Sir,

Conscious that your time is much occupied, I feel a great repugnance in intruding my present request; but Letitia's anxiety for your opinion will, I am afraid, make you consider us both very troublesome. Without your sanction she feels herself without a hope of success, and has no resolution to go on. She has upon her list more than sufficient to defray the expenses of publication—I do not mean by subscription.

Mrs. Siddons is shortly going to Oxford, and as we have connections there, and Mrs. S. is taking it up very warmly, we have hope that something may be done for our poetic sketches. A line from you, giving her your opinion, will settle the matter, whether she may proceed.

I am, dear sir,
Very gratefully yours,
C. J. Landon.

It is not clear what exactly is meant by "something may be done" for the "poetic sketches," since sufficient subsidies for the book seem already to have been obtained; perhaps there was a thought of finding a publisher in Oxford, where L.E.L.'s uncle, Whittington Landon, was Provost of Worcester College. Or perhaps this refers to a separate collection of poems, including some of the "poetical sketches" that were published in *The Literary Gazette* beginning in September 1821. In any case, after this, Jerdan remarks, the "minor pieces to fill up the volume were definitely arranged,"[31] and the plan for publication went ahead, helped by a financial contribution from the author's grandmother, and by the dedication to her friend, the famous actress, Mrs. Siddons (née Sarah Kemble; 1755-1831), whose respected name undoubtedly helped secure the polite reception of the volume. There is a connection of sorts with the title poem, since Mrs. Siddons traveled to Switzerland in 1821 to visit her brother, John Kemble.[32]

The publisher of *The Fate of Adelaide*, John Warren, of Old Bond Street, London, is far less well known than contemporaries of his like Constable, Murray, Longman, or Colburn, but he had a moderately substantial list, since no less than twenty-nine titles of his are advertised in *The Literary Gazette* for 1821, several of them in second or third printings. The range of subjects and genres is broad,

INTRODUCTION

but the preponderance are literary titles, some by more or less prominent figures of the time, such as: George Croly, "Barry Cornwall" (pen name of B. W. Procter), John Banim, and William Hazlitt, whose *Lectures on the Dramatic Literature of the Age of Elizabeth*, and *A View of the English Stage*, and volume one of *Table-Talk* were published by Warren.[33]

Some of the principal titles of 1821, as reflected in review articles in *The Literary Gazette*, were: *Kenilworth*, by "The Great Unknown," in January, and in December, *The Pirate*; in between, *Memoirs of the Life of Anne Boleyn*, by Miss Benger; *Metrical Legends of Exalted Characters*, by Joanna Baillie; *The Mountain Bard*, by James Hogg, "The Ettrick Shepherd" (third edition, greatly enlarged; first published in 1807); *A Vision of Judgment*, by Southey; Lady Morgan's *Italy*; *Ten Years' Exile*, by Madame de Staël; Byron's *Cain, Sardanapalus, and The Two Foscari,* and *Don Juan*, cantos iii, iv, and v; and *The Village Minstrel*, by John Clare.

Amid such company, L. E. Landon's volume of verse appeared in August and was treated not as a "vanity" publication but as a regularly issued work, advertised or announced not only in *The Literary Gazette*, but also in other important journals, such as *The Quarterly Review, Blackwood's Magazine,* and *The Edinburgh Review*.[34] A lengthy review article appeared in *The Literary Gazette*, unsigned, but surely by Jerdan; and a brief notice in *The New Monthly Magazine*.[35] Both publications were controlled by Henry Colburn, so Jerdan could have had an opportunity of recommending the book to the *New Monthly*. Jerdan's review begins:

> This, amid the number of works of the same character, which issue with such fertility from the press, has attracted our notice, not merely by its being the production of a youthful female pen, but by its possessing poetic merits of a very pleasing order. The critic will, no doubt, perceive in it those features which are common to inexperienced writers, and some that are rather peculiar to the fair sex. Exuberance of fancy, inequality of diction, and the lingering of partial fondness on images of beauty and nature, are obvious in the ideas and style. But there are touches worthy of more matured talent, and of genius more patiently cultivated; and as a first effort, we consider this little volume to offer far greater promise than is usual in similar performances by young ladies, whose fine tastes, or sometimes warmed imaginations, lead them to court the muses.

He then summarizes the poem, illustrating it with generous quotations,[36] and concludes:

> These extracts will, we trust, justify the praise we have bestowed upon this volume, and encourage its trembling author to more measured flights. She has the feeling and genius of poesy in her mind, and if she cultivates its mechanical requisites, represses words, cherishes deep-thinking, and ponders on selection and polish, will, we doubt not, add one other ornament to the brilliant and delightful train of British female bards.

The review ends with reprints of a selection from the "minor poems" in the book: "Absence" (p. 75), "Sonnet" (p. 83), "Stanzas" (p. 85), and "The Phoenix and the Dove" (p. 115).

The author of the notice in *The New Monthly Magazine*, is more outspoken in criticism, but at the same time generous in praise; the review is short enough to quote in its entirety:

> In some touches the authoress of this poem reminds us of those works which have gained so much fame to the youthful bard who has chosen to stand forth as a candidate for it under the assumed name of Barry Cornwall. In point of exciting strong interest, however, she is not so fortunate: the story of her principal poem contains nothing that is new, and little that is striking; it draws the reader on solely by its descriptions and reflections, which would produce just as much effect if they were detached from the narrative altogether. In the minor pieces this fault is not so evident. A single sentiment, or a single image, clothed in harmonious numbers, and illustrated in the compass of a few lines, can only afford pleasure, and must excite admiration unmixed with any of that severity of criticism which the authoress deprecates with an interesting modesty, and which most assuredly will never be excited by a performance unassuming and elegant as the present.

The reviewer for *The New Monthly Magazine* points out a characteristic that applies not only to the volume under consideration, but to all of L.E.L.'s poetry, and to much of her fiction: the supremacy of her lyric intensity and corresponding deficiency of narrative interest in her longer works (one would except her novel

INTRODUCTION

Ethel Churchill). The characters seldom come to life as individuals, and seldom attract the reader for their own sake. The point is also made by Jules Le Fèvre-Deumier, the only critic to discuss *The Fate of Adelaide* in any detail.[37] The explanation is, it seems to me, simply that her principal subject was initially—and throughout her work remained—herself. In this sense she is a typical "romantic" poet, for whom the only subject, the only reality, is the self. If this is at the root of her weakness in narrative, it is correspondingly one of the sources of her strength as a lyric poet. But it is a commonplace observation that intensity of feeling does not alone suffice for perfection of artistry. What one sees in her poetry is the result of a natural gift of lyric composition that was a perfect vehicle for the expression of her intensely felt intellectual and emotional experience.

The Fate of Adelaide does not appear in the collected editions of L.E.L.'s works; and W. B. Scott, in the "Memoir" to the 1873 volume (reprinted by Scholars' Facsimiles & Reprints, with an introduction and additional poems, 1990) dismisses it as "very juvenile." One doubts if he ever set eyes on a copy of it, for what is most striking is not so much its juvenility as its maturity. Had she never written anything else, it would remain an interesting collection of poems; but looking backward with the knowledge of her subsequent literary career, one cannot help being struck by finding so many of the themes and so much of the manner of her later work in this first volume of hers. Le Fèvre-Deumier says of it: "Elle est déjà là tout entière"; this is of course a deliberate overstatement, but there is more than a grain of truth in his words.

The title poem is obviously cut from the same pattern as her later narratives. Like them, it is a love story, with, as in Madame de Staël's *Corinne*, an eternal triangle, consisting of two women and a man, and the outcome is death or despair for everybody. One may smile at the triteness of the romantic clichés, as L.E.L. herself does in her letter to her cousin, quoted above. But even though she was able to make fun of her poem's tragic close, she was also serious about it. Her ambivalence is, to me at any rate, one of her most attractive qualities as a writer. She worshipped beauty and nature and art and poetry and love and at the same time felt that it was all nonsense—nothing more than passionate feelings of enthusiasm that make one momentarily forget that life as a whole is a lonely struggle for material survival. From such a perspective, illusion, for Landon, is the only thing that makes it possible to go on living, and illusion is none the less precious for the awareness of its falsity; in fact, the knowledge that false illusions are all one has makes them all the more precious. As Shakespeare expresses it in sonnet 138, "love's best habit is in seeming trust." Such cynicism is a romantic commonplace too, but none the less, for Landon, I believe, a deeply felt truth. One tends to see in her later poems expressions of her disillusionment with the bitter fruit of her literary success, but one is surprised to find kindred sentiments expressed here in poems like her *i libellum* or *envoi*, "The Farewell" (p. 69), and "To ———" (p. 95), and "The Star" (p. 117), published as she stood, at the age of eighteen, on the threshold of fulfilling her artistic aspirations.

Similarly, knowing her later history, one is not surprised at the ironic presentation of love in her mature poetry. But again, one finds similar expressions in this collection, as in "Love's Parting Wreath" and "Answer" (pp. 103-106), as well as in the title poem. The similarity between her early and her mature writing is perhaps most strikingly seen as one compares two of her last poems—"The Polar Star" and "Night at Sea," which were written on board ship as she sailed to Africa in 1838—with the two poems titled "Absence" (pp. 75 & 110), and especially with "Lines to ———" (p. 70).

Returning to the contemporary reviewers of *The Fate of Adelaide*, one must agree that, in spite of the faults of construction in the title poem, and the general conventionality of diction and versification, the book as a whole possesses a richness of imagination that gives it rewarding moments, and offers great promise for a talent that was essentially lyrical—less interested in narrative and character than in observation, and, most of all, in the poetic expression of feelings.

Apparently the book had reasonably successful sales, all things considered, but Warren went out of business within weeks of its publication.[38] From a twentieth-century vantage point one might be inclined to attribute his business reversal to his taking on such books as the first volume of poems by L. E. Landon. But the publishing business was then, as it is now, a matter of the moment, and L.E.L. was in fact, as the sequel proved, an excellent prospect—a talented author with the backing of an influential figure such as Jerdan was; and in due course her poems, later published by Longman, were highly successful both critically and monetarily. If anything, Warren's taking on of this project indicates his good instincts as a publisher. On the other hand, publishing was a risky business: modern systems of promotion, production, and distribution were making the appearance of massive best-sellers possible, but such sales required a massive and of necessity highly leveraged capital investment;[39] an unexpected turn of events could throw the whole venture into calamity, as no case shows better than that of Sir Walter Scott, one of the biggest bestsellers in literary history, whose publisher, Constable, in the midst of unparalleled prosperity, suddenly went bankrupt in 1826, leaving debts of more than a hundred thousand pounds.

L.E.L.'s little book sold well enough to earn her £50, part or all which must have represented a refund of the amount of the subsidy; but because of Warren's collapse, she never collected a penny of it.[40] However, the publication was ultimately a success, since the sales and reviews, in Jerdan's words, "placed the gifted author in a position to negotiate for and receive considerable sums for all her subsequent works."[41]

Between her first publications in *The Literary Gazette* in 1820, and the publication of *The Fate of Adelaide* in August 1821, L.E.L. had remained in the background as a writer, although at least one poem of hers appeared, in total anonymity, without even a single initial as a signature.[42] But on 22 September 1821, in No. 244 of *The Literary Gazette*, the "three magical letters" *L.E.L.* made their debut, appended to a poem titled "Bells," and to "Stanzas On the Death of Miss Campbell." In subsequent issues, other poems followed over this signature, which soon became the focus of a cult, among whose adherents were figures as diverse as the young Edward Bulwer and the Quaker poet, Bernard Barton, who in February 1822 apostrophized the author as follows:

> I know not who, or what, thou art,
>   Nor do I seek to know thee,
> Whilst thou, performing thus thy part,
>   Such banquets can bestow me.
> Then be, as long as thou shalt list,
> My viewless, nameless melodist.[43]

Writing in 1831, Bulwer recalled:

> We remember well when she first appeared before the public in the pages of "The Literary Gazette." We were at that time more capable than we are now of poetic enthusiasm; and certainly that enthusiasm we not only felt ourselves, but we shared with every second person we then met. We were young, and at college, lavishing our golden years, not so much on the Greek verse and

INTRODUCTION

> mystic character to which we ought, perhaps, to have been rigidly devoted, as "Our heart in passion and our head in rhymes." At that time, poetry was not yet out of fashion, at least with us of the cloister; and there was always, in the Reading Room of the Union, a rush every Saturday afternoon for "The Literary Gazette," and an impatient anxiety to hasten at once to that corner of the sheet which contained the three magical letters of "L.E.L." And all of us praised the verse, and all of us guessed at the author. We soon learned it was a female, and our admiration was doubled, and our conjectures tripled. Was she young? Was she pretty? and—for there were some embryo fortune-hunters among us—was she rich?[44]

This somewhat highly colored account says more about the young dandy that Bulwer was then than about the poet. But there is no question that Bulwer's enthusiasm was shared by many. "L.E.L." became a regular contributor to almost every issue of *The Literary Gazette*, not only as a palindromic initialist poet, but also as an anonymous author of book reviews. Soon she began contributing to gift books like *Forget Me Not* (first issued in late 1822; dated 1823). And her second volume of poems, *The Improvisatrice* (July 1824) was an unqualified success, rapidly running through six editions and earning the author the impressive sum of £300. "L.E.L." was truly launched on the remarkable literary career that had begun with *The Fate of Adelaide*.

F. J. Sypher

New York, New York

INTRODUCTION

NOTES

1. The connection with "Sir William Landon, Knt." is stated by Laman Blanchard in *Life and Literary Remains of L.E.L.* (London, 1841), vol. 1, p. 1, perhaps from data provided by the poet's brother, W. H. Landon, or by her cousin, Elizabeth Landon. Blanchard identifies the poet's great-grandfather as John (son of William), rather than as Thomas; but more confidence is inspired by the information from contemporary documents quoted by Joseph Foster in *Alumni Oxonienses*, vol. 3 (1715-1886) (Kraus Reprint, 1968), p. 813. The poet's father's birth year is derived from the original manuscript entry in the parish register at the Church of St. James the Great, Tedstone Delamere, which records family baptisms as follows: Jenny, 16 April 1754; John, 7 March 1756; Whittington, 12 September 1758; Thomas, 15 May 1762; James, 2 November 1764; Elizabeth, 17 September 1769. These transcripts were kindly provided by the Reverend R. J. Colby, Rector of Tedstone Delamere. Also recorded is the burial of the Reverend John Landon, 2 September 1782.

2. J. O. Landon, *Landon Genealogy* (New York, 1928), pp. 8-9.

3. Biographical notice of L.E.L. in *The Book of Gems: The Modern Poets and Artists of Great Britain*, edited by S. C. Hall (London, 1838), p. 178; based on information provided by the poet, who was a close friend of the editor and of Anna Maria Hall (see below, note 16). Details on John Landon's service would probably be contained in Admiralty Records at the Public Record Office at Kew.

4. On Admiral Bowyer, see the *Dictionary of National Biography*, and sources referred to there. His voyages may offer clues to John Landon's service.

5. "Memoir" of L.E.L. in an edition of her novel, *Romance and Reality* (London, 1848), p. viii. Internal evidence identifies William Jerdan as the unnamed author.

6. Chapter on L.E.L. by Katharine Byerly Thomson and J. C. Thomson (writing under the pseudonyms, "Grace & Philip Wharton") in *The Queens of Society* (New York, 1890; first pub. 1860), vol. 1, pp. 160-201. Cf. the account in K. B. Thomson's *Recollections of Literary Characters and Celebrated Places* (London, 1854), vol. 2, pp. 67-98. Mrs. Thomson's accounts have special value because they are based on long and close friendship; her husband, Dr. Anthony Todd Thomson, was L.E.L.'s physician.

7. See Dorothy Stroud, *Henry Holland: His Life and Architecture* (London, 1966), pp. 43-49 and accompanying illustrations. There is an

attractive print of "Sloane Place," later known as "The Pavilion," showing the lake and island, in Thomas Faulkner's *An Historical and Topographical Description of Chelsea and its Environs* (London, 1810), facing p. 434. See also K. B. Thomson in *The Queens of Society* cited above. The original houses of Hans Place were later replaced by the late Victorian style structures that may be seen there today. On the literary associations of the neighborhood, see George G. Williams, *Guide to Literary London* (London, 1973; repr. 1988), pp. 265-266.

8. Quoted, by permission, from a manuscript copy in the author's hand, in the Henry W. and Albert A. Berg Collection, The New York Public Library, Astor, Lenox and Tilden Foundations. The poem appears to have been set to music (K. B. Thomson, *The Queens of Society*, vol. 1, p. 172), and was undoubtedly published, but I have not located the printed text or the score of the musical setting. L.E.L. studied music with Miss Bisset, to whom one of the poems in the present collection is dedicated (p. 135); see *The Queens of Society*, vol. 2, p. 165, and Blanchard, vol. 1, p. 11.

9. For details, see Constance Hill, *Mary Russell Mitford and Her Surroundings* (London, 1920), pp. 63-88; Marjorie Astin, *Mary Russell Mitford: Her Circle and Her Books* (London, 1930), pp. 22-24; W. J. Roberts, *Mary Russell Mitford: The Tragedy of a Blue Stocking* (London, 1913), pp. 40-64.

10. See Henry Blyth, *Caro, The Fatal Passion: The Life of Lady Caroline Lamb* (London, 1972), pp. 24-26. See also *Lady Bessborough and Her Family Circle*, edited by The Earl of Bessborough, with A. Aspinall (London, 1940), with a striking portrait of Lady Caroline Lamb facing p. 212.

11. K. B. Thomson, *The Queens of Society*, vol. 1, p. 164.

12. See the *Victoria History of the Counties of England: Middlesex*, vol. 4 (1971), pp. 150 (map), 157; vol. 5 (1976), pp. 4 (map), 21. Cf. Blanchard, vol. 1, p. 8. On agriculture in the period, see Charles Singer, et al., *A History of Technology*, 5 vols. (Oxford, 1954-58), vol. 4, pp. 1-43.

13. On Trevor Park, see the *Victoria History of the Counties of England: Hertfordshire*, vol. 2 (1908; repr. 1971), p. 338; F. C. Cass, *East Barnet* (Westminster, 1885-92), pp. 44-69; J. E. Cussans, *History of Hertfordshire* (London, 1870-81), vol. 3, part 2, p. 62; Daniel Lysons, *The Environs of London*, 2d ed. (London, 1791), vol. 1, part 2, pp. 759, 766. On Lord Trevor, see *DNB*. Cass had been informed that the house was "an ancient gabled structure"; so far I have not been

INTRODUCTION

able to find a picture of it.

14. Arabella Stuart was a figure of interest in the nineteenth century, and several biographies of her have appeared; see especially P. M. Handover, *Arbella Stuart* (London, 1957), with its detailed bibliography. Cf. the poem by Felicia Hemans, "Arabella Stuart," the opening piece of *Records of Woman* (1828).

15. *Merchant Taylors' School Register 1561-1934*, edited by Mrs. E. P. Hart (London, 1936), vol. 2, under W. H. Landon (unpaged). See also Foster, loc. cit. in n. 1 above.

16. This quotation is from L.E.L.'s letter to S. C. Hall, used by him in writing the biographical sketch in *The Book of Gems* (see n. 3 above); the full text of the letter is in Hall's *A Book of Memories of Great Men and Women of the Age*, 2d ed. (London, 1877; first pub. 1871), pp. 269-70. See also the article by the Halls, "Memories of Authors," *The Atlantic Monthly*, vol. 15 (1865), pp. 330-40. *The Book of Gems* includes L.E.L.'s poem "Red Riding Hood," where she sees a type of her own country girlhood, pp. 179-81. See the description of L.'s favorite haunt—the pond with its willow and island—in her autobiographical story, "The History of a Child," in *Traits and Trials of Early Life* (1836).

17. Blanchard, vol. 1, p. 9.

18. The book was probably: *The Life of Petrarch Collected from Mémoires pour la vie de Petrarch*, by Susannah Dobson (d. 1795; see *DNB*), first published, London, 1775, and often reprinted.

19. Letter to S. C. Hall, cited above, n. 16.

20. Blanchard, vol. 1, p. 18.

21. On *Sylvester Tramper*, see D. E. Enfield, *L.E.L. A Mystery of the Thirties* (London, 1928), pp. 38-41. *The Arabian Nights* appeared in several editions at this time, e.g., one in 4 vols. (like the set recalled in "The History of a Child"), London, 1811, translated from the French of Galland by G. S. Beaumont.

22. Op. cit., n. 5 above, p. ix.

23. J. W. Fortescue, *A History of the British Army*, vol. 11 (1815-1838) (London, 1923), pp. 46-47. See also Singer, *A History of Technology*, vol. 4, p. 22.

24. Letter to S. C. Hall, cited above, n. 16.

25. *The Autobiography of William Jerdan*, 4 vols. (London, 1852-53); see Vol. 3, pp. 168-206 on L.E.L.; the quotation is from p. 174.

26. Elizabeth Landon's polite letters are printed in Jerdan's *Autobiography*, vol. 3, pp. 175-76.

27. Jerdan, op. cit., n. 5 above, p. xi.

INTRODUCTION

28. L.E.L.'s seven publications in *The Literary Gazette* in 1820 were: "Rome" (No. 164, 11 March, p. 173); "The Michaelmas Daisy" (No. 165, 18 March, p. 190); "A West Indian Anecdote, Versified" (No. 185, 5 August, p. 507); "Fragment" (No. 188, 26 August, pp. 556-57); "Vaucluse," and untitled lines beginning: "The bee, when varying flowers are nigh" (No. 196, 21 October, p. 685); Sonnet ("There is Shape, upon whose wrinkled brow") (No. 200, 18 November, p. 746). Two of these poems were reprinted in *The Fate of Adelaide*; see the "Bibliographical Note" below.

29. This letter by L.E.L. and the following two letters by her mother, are printed by Jerdan, *Autobiography*, vol. 3, pp. 181-82. There seems to be an error in the letter dated Wednesday Nov. 4th, since the 4th fell on a Saturday in 1820; probably it should read either Nov. 1st or Nov. 8th. Coaching time from Bristol to London was a mere two days, which helps estimate the time it would have taken for letters to go back and forth; see Mary Alden Hopkins, *Hannah More and Her Circle* (New York & Toronto, 1947), p. 19.

30. This and the following letter by L.E.L. are printed by Blanchard, vol. 1, pp. 27-28 & 35-37 (the ellipses are his).

31. *Autobiography*, vol. 3, p. 182.

32. Yvonne Ffrench, *Mrs. Siddons: Tragic Actress* (London, 1936, repr. 1954), p. 239.

33. Advertisements of Hazlitt's works appear in *The Literary Gazette*, 1821: No. 214 (24 February), p. 128; No. 221 (14 April), p. 240. See also: P. P. Howe, *The Life of William Hazlitt* (New York, 1923), pp. 290, 310, & 366-67; Geoffrey Keynes, *Bibliography of William Hazlitt* (London, 1931), pp. 31, 51, 52, 54.

34. *The Literary Gazette*, No. 241 (1 September 1821), p. 560; *Quarterly Review*, vol. 26 (October 1821), p. 275; *Blackwood's Magazine*, vol. 10, No. 57 (November 1821), p. 482; *Edinburgh Review*, vol. 36 (February 1822), p. 571.

35. *The Literary Gazette*, No. 237 (4 August 1821), pp. 483-84; *New Monthly Magazine*, vol. 3 (New Series), part 3 (1 November 1821), p. 579. Not one to miss an opportunity, L.E.L., on seeing this review, shot off three poems for the consideration of the editor—then Thomas Campbell, with Cyrus Redding as his assistant—with a brief accompanying letter, dated 4 November (MS. Berg collection, The New York Public Library). They do not appear to have been accepted, but in later years she became a regular contributor to the journal.

36. The quotations are from pp. 14, 25, 27-28, 58, 60, 65, and 66.

INTRODUCTION

37. "Létitia Elisabeth Landon," in *Célébrités anglaises* (Paris, 1895), pp. 227-309. The discussion of *Adelaide* appears on pp. 234-38.

38. K. B. Thomson, *Recollections*, vol. 2, p. 74; P. P. Howe, *The Life of William Hazlitt*, pp. 366-67. After 1 September there are no further advertisements by Warren in *The Literary Gazette*.

39. See John Feather, *A History of British Publishing* (London, 1988), pp. 150-51.

40. K. B. Thomson, *Recollections*, vol. 2, p. 74. At the advertised retail price of 7s. 6d. per copy, £50 would represent gross sales of 133 copies; allowing for costs, discounts, refund of subsidy, and profits, one would conclude that several hundred copies of the book had been sold.

41. *Autobiography*, vol. 3, p. 180.

42. "Apologue. The thought Suggested by a Spanish saying: 'Air Fire–Water–Shame'," *The Literary Gazette*, No. 238 (11 August 1821), p. 509. Reprinted in *The Improvisatrice* (1824).

43. Quoted by Blanchard, vol. 1, p. 31.

44. Review (unsigned) of L.E.L.'s first novel, *Romance and Reality*, in *The New Monthly Magazine*, vol. 32 (New Series), part 2 (December 1831), pp. 545-51; the quoted passage is on pp. 546-47.

INTRODUCTION

BIBLIOGRAPHICAL NOTE

The present reprint is made, by permission, from the copy in The British Library (shelfmark 994.f21). There is also a copy in the Bodleian Library at Oxford, and one in the Cambridge University Library, and one is listed as being at the University of Edinburgh. The sole copy listed in *The National Union Catalogue, Pre-1956 Imprints* is reported as "missing." Two apparent oversights in the book require mention. In Canto II, the numbering of the sections omits the number IX (pp. 48-50). At the end of the volume, a note to the poem titled "Fragment" (p. 149) refers to it as "the only Poem in the volume previously published"–it appeared in *The Literary Gazette*, No. 188 (26 August 1820), pp. 556-57. However, the lines titled "Addressed to ———" (p. 154) also appeared, untitled, in the same journal, No. 196 (21 October 1820), p. 685. So far as I know, this is the first reprint of the text since its original publication in 1821.

ACKNOWLEDGMENTS

An expression of grateful appreciation is due to all who contributed advice or information for this edition of *The Fate of Adelaide*: especially to the many libraries and librarians in the U.S.A. and in Britain who answered inquiries and made material available for consultation; particularly to The British Library and to The New York Public Library for the permissions noted elsewhere in this introduction; to the Reverend R. J. Colby for unpublished data recorded in note 1; to the Reverend H. E. Steed, of East Barnet, and to Mrs. Gillian Gear, M.A., Hon. Secretary of the Barnet & District Local History Society, for information about Trevor Park; to Scholars' Facsimiles & Reprints for undertaking this publication; to Rudolph Ellenbogen, Nicholas D. Ward, and Henry Weldon for advice and encouragement of many kinds; and to Peggy Kirby, who died on 11 March 1989, whose knowledge and love of poetry–*L'Amor che move il sole e l'altre stelle*–have been an inspiration.

22 Hans Place

45 Brompton Row

William Jerdan, by Maclise

Mrs. Siddons, by Downman

THE
FATE OF ADELAIDE,

A SWISS ROMANTIC TALE;

AND

OTHER POEMS:

BY

LETITIA ELIZABETH LANDON.

LONDON:
JOHN WARREN, OLD BOND STREET.
MDCCCXXI.

TO MRS. SIDDONS.

Madam,

The sanction of a Lady so long distinguished for brilliant talents, has to me, indeed, been the greatest encouragement. Ever accustomed to look up to Mrs. Siddons as the perfection of all that is beautiful and sublime in poetry, I cannot express how gratified I feel in being allowed to bring my first offering to a shrine so much venerated. However unworthy I may be of the high honour conferred, it could not be more gratefully appreciated than by one, whose admiration and respect, can, Madam, only be equalled by her gratitude.

L. E. L.

PREFACE.

THE appeal of so young a Candidate for public favour as myself, must be made less to the candour, than to the kindness of my judges. Well aware that, like the fountain of youth of which we read in the Fairy Tales of the East, the bright springs of poetry may be drank but by few; and that the path we fondly deemed led to immortality, too often terminates in the waters of oblivion—I dare only intreat gentle visitings, for the slight plant thus adventured in open daylight; and look forward to its fate with fear, rather than with hope that it will blossom to maturity.

THE FATE OF ADELAIDE.

CANTO I.

Romantic Switzerland! thy scenes are traced
With characters of strange wild loveliness,
Beauty and desolation, side by side;
Here lofty rocks uprise, where nature seems
To dwell alone in silent majesty;
Rob'd by the snow, her stately palace fram'd
Of the white hills; towering in all their pride,
The frost's gigantic mounds are lost in clouds,

Like to vast castles rear'd in middle air.
The ice has sculptur'd too strange imagery—
Obelisks, columns, spires, fantastic piles;
Some like the polish'd marble, others clear
As the rock crystal, others sparkling with
The hues that melt along the sunborn bow.
And winter frowns upon the throne, which he
Has been whole ages raising, and beneath,
The gloomy vallies, like his footstool lie,
Where summer never comes—where never spring
Wreathes the young flowers round her golden hair.
The sun looks forth in beauty, but in vain,
Those dark vales never know the light of noon:
But there they hide them in their sullenness,
As the pale spirit of desolation chose
Them for his lonely haunt. No trace hath been
Of living thing upon those untrack'd snows;
Nought hath pass'd o'er them but the printless
  wind;

Ev'n that wild deer, which loves the mountain side,
Springs the abyss, and dares the venturous path
We shrink to look upon, yet comes not here.
For perilous were the rocks, and the false ice
Were slippery as the friendships of this life—
When most we lean on them, most treach'rous then,
Smooth but deceiving; and the precipice
Yawns in its fearful darkness close beneath;
So close, that but a single step aside,
And human help were vanity indeed!
And o'er them lowers destruction, high in air,
Upon those jutting crags, whose rugged sides,
Riven in fragments, and like ruins pil'd,
Seem as that giants of those ancient days
When earthborn creatures braved th' Olympic Gods,
Those of whom fable tells, had torn away
Rocks from their solid base, and with strong arm,
Parted the mountains: there the avalanche hangs,

Mighty, but tremulous ; just a light breath
Will loosen it from off it's airy throne ;
Then down it hurls in wrath, like to the sound
Of thunder amid storms, or as the voice
Of rushing waters—death in its career.
The lurking tempests hold their gathering place
Within these caves, waiting the angry winds
Which are to bear their terrors thro' the skies.
But 'mid these scenes of wintry gloom, are some
Fair relics of the spring time blossoms, like
The sunny smiles of May, as if some breeze,
Just wander'd from delightful Italy,
Had brought the blessings of its birth-place here.
And lovely are the vallies which extend
Beneath the mountains ; oh ! how sweet it is
To gaze around when summer sunset sheds
Its splendor in the west ; when the bright clouds,
Warm with the hues of eve, gleam o'er the sky,
As 'twere some heavenly spirit veil'd his form

In bursts of glory from a mortal eye.
When glowing in the ray, the glacier's shine,
With all the opal's varied colouring,
And every tint that tulip beds disclose,
Gilds the rich pageantry of parting day;
The golden arches, rich with purple gems,
Pillars of light, and crimson colonnades,
Like the gay palaces of fairy land
Which flit upon the thought, when the young eye
Dwells in rapt wonder on the enchanted tale.
Beneath are sun-bright vales and silver lakes,
The blue waves mantled with reflected red,
The sky's bright image on the stream imprest;
Green vineyards wreathing round the steep hill's side,
And groups of cheerful peasantry reclin'd
By their white dwellings, round whose lowly thatch
The light laburnum waves her yellow hair;
And rising on the gale, is heard the sound
Of rustic music, of that cherish'd song

The Switzer loves ; whose every note is fraught
With thoughts of love, youth, home, and happiness.

II.

Raised on a rock, which overlooks the vale,
Like to it's guardian power, a ruin stands ;
It is o'ergrown with ivy, and the walls,
Mouldering around, are grey with aged moss.
There is yet left one melancholy hall—
The roof is riven, and the big rain drops beat
Upon the weed-grown floor ; and sun-beams fall,
Almost in mockery, for they are fraught
With too much happiness for scenes like this.
It has no tapestry but the spider's web ;
No music save the skreech owl's fearful cry,
And the bat's noisy flight, or when the wind
Howls thro' it drearily, as 'twere a dirge

Mourning it's fallen fortunes. Ask it's fate
Of those who dwell around, and they will tell
The wild romantic tales of other days—
Remembrances that linger like the tints
Of evening blushes 'neath the veil of night.
Such is the tale of which my lyre would tell,
(Unskill'd and plaintive are the notes it breathes,)
I scarce may hope to catch one echo'd sound,
One murmur of the strain I love so well.
My wreath, if wreath at all my harp may claim,
Will be of simplest field-flowers. Oh! belov'd
Inspirer of thy youthful minstrel's dream,
How dear the meed of fame would be to me!
For thou must see it, and thy hand would give
The brightest blossom that could sparkle there.
Thine was the earliest smile that ever shed
Its cheering light on my young laurel's growth.
Tho' other praise be dear (where is the bard,
To whom the voice of flattery is not sweet?)

Yet never, never can approval's smile
Be half so treasur'd, half so priz'd as thine.

III.

It was a night of gloom; strange shadowy forms
Rode on the dreary wind, which hoarsely blew
A prelude to the tempest's gathering.
Darkness was on the sky, and murky shades
Obscur'd the brightness of the rising moon,
Which, struggling, threw at times a silvery smile,
Soon disappearing, and rebellious clouds
Crowded around and mock'd their gentle queen;
The stars were hidden; one, and one alone,
Shed o'er the west her solitary ray;
And well that one might linger;—it had been,
In days which have a hallow'd memory,
The star peculiar to the smiling pow'r
Of love and beauty: never more than now

Could it seem Woman's emblem; so her light
Should shine 'mid darkness, and her loveliness
Cheer the dull hour of gloom :—e'en that is past,
A cloud like death came over it, and quench'd
Its tender beam; at once the storm pour'd forth
Its cup of fury, and the blasts arose,
Sweeping among the mountains with a sound
Of anger and of anguish, laughter, groans,
And shrieks as if of torture, and deep sobs
Mingled together; and at times the voice
Of thunder spake in wrath; and crashing woods,
Fierce gusts, and echoing caves, dread answers
    gave.
The Spirit of the lightning fiercely roll'd
His eyes of fire athwart the sky, and rent
The veil of blackness with his burning glance.
Dark lower'd the fearful night, but onwards still
The traveller urg'd his course; there was no light
To point the gloomy path, save when a flash

Glar'd its blue flame around.   The wood is past,
And he has gain'd the steep ascent which leads
To Ethlin's Castle.——He has entered now ;—
'Tis a young warrior, and his bosom wears
The red-cross.   Instant cries of joy arise,
And words of greeting; one to meet him sprang,
And clasp'd him in her arms, while his warm cheek
Was wet with her sweet tears of tenderness—
My brother! oh, my brother! welcome home.
She started back, half sorrow half surprise,
From his averted clasp, and on him gaz'd
Almost reproachfully ; and then her glance
Fell on a stranger's form : she turn'd and hid
Her gathering blushes in her father's arms.
The stranger spoke no word, but gave an urn
Unto that venerable chieftain's hand.
It told its tale too well ; the dear, the lost,
For whom their lips yet trembled with the words
Of fond affection hailing his return,

He was gone from them, and the gates of death
Had clos'd for ever on their earthly love.

IV.

Most heavily this blight fell on the heart
Of Ethlin's Lord.   Ernest had been his pride ;
On whom each bosom hope had built its throne;
With what proud joy the warrior sire had mark'd
The promise of his boyhood, when a child,
A very infant in his nurse's arms,
His eye would sparkle at the trumpet's voice,
And his young cheek grow red, when tales were
    told
Of glorious battle and heroic deeds !
It came, the wish'd-for time, and Ernest took
His father's sword, and sought the fields of war.
When Europe pour'd her thousands on the East,
That sword was claim'd by no unworthy hand :

Again it flash'd the reddest in the fight—
It was a hero's still! But all too soon;
Cropt in his spring of glory, Ernest fell.——
In that lone moment, when all earthly ties
More fond, more holy, twine around the heart,
He thought upon his home; and in that thought
There was a chill more terrible than death,
He gaz'd upon the chief, who knelt beside,
And cool'd his burning lips with the fresh spring,
And held his dying brow—" Orlando, we
Together sought these fatal plains, and still
Our course has been together, and our swords
Have been as one: oh! by thy love for me,
And by thy faith, let not my ashes mix
With this accursed earth; but let them rest
Their last sad sleep in my own Switzerland!
My spirit would not slumber in a grave,
On which a father's blessing was not breath'd—
That was not moisten'd by my sister's tears.

Orlando, thou wilt tell them, that my **death**
Was such as well became a hero's child!"

V.

How precious is the memory of those
Who slumber in the tomb! their lightest word
And look is then recall'd, and hallowed
As tender relics love had left behind—
Sweet but sad treasures! ah, how dear the thought
Which dwells on those departed; when the heart
Beats quick with fond reflections, and the worth,
The praise of those gone to their silent sleep,
Comes like a healing balm to sorrow's wound.
Most soothing was it to the father's grief
To hear how gloriously his Ernest fell;
Still would he ask Orlando of the fields
Which they had fought together; and the tale,
Tho' often told, was sweet unto his ear,
As the blithe peal, that tells the traveller,

Wayworn and faint, a refuge is at hand.——
And there was one who listened to the tale,
And treasur'd ev'ry word Orlando breathed.
Young Adelaide, those accents are to thee
As sounds of heav'nly music, which no time
Or change can ever banish from the heart!

VI.

Oh, love! how exquisite thy visions are!
Spring of the soul, what flowers can equal thine?
When every other virtue fled from earth,
Thou linger'dst still, last solace of our path.
What were the world, bereft of thee?—a void,
Without one sunny place on which the eye
Might rest for sweet refreshment. Thou art not
A summer blossom only; it is thine
To bloom in beauty on the wint'ry hour:
When storms and sorrows press the spirit down,

Then dost thou come, a gentle comforter,
Tenderly binding up the broken heart.—
Celestial thy first dawning! it is like
The Morn awakening the smiling Hours,
Calling the flowers from their fragrant dreams,
And breathing melody and perfume around.
So does thy influence brighten on the soul,
Waking it to a new enchanted world,
Where every thought is gladness.

      Never yet
Hath love dwelt in a lovelier temple than
That youthful maiden's form: she had now reach'd
Youth's fairest season, when the opening flower
Is just between the green bud and full rose.
There was a melancholy beauty in
The deep blue of her eyes;—'twas sad, yet soft,
Melting in tenderness 'neath the dark lash
That curtain'd its mild splendor; ev'ry glance
Bespoke a spirit wild and fanciful,—

A heart that answer'd sorrow's slightest thrill;
And thoughts that dwelt not on reality,
But lov'd to wander in imagin'd scenes,
'Mid fancy's fair creation revelling.
A tender bloom just dawn'd upon her cheek,
Too pale, to say the rose was glowing there,
But the soft hue which the white violet
Wears on its perfum'd leaf; save when a blush
Deepen'd to crimson radiance o'er her face.
Her voice was sweet as the last dying close
Waked from the wild guitar in Spanish groves,
When the fond lover pours his soul in song,
And echo answers like a maiden's sigh.
It had those silvery tones which, lingering, hang
Upon the ear, and melt into the heart.
Young, lovely with the sunny brow of youth,
More touching from the pensive shade which threw
A magic charm around it. Such she was,
Fair as the spring time of her native vales.

I need not say how sweet the accents fell,
When first Orlando told his tale of love—
How tender was the blush that welcom'd it;
Nor need I tell how happy were the hours
That pass'd away in love's enchanted dreams;
'Twas all the bard e'er feign'd, or young hearts felt,
Of joys, like spring days, bright and fugitive.——
But not long in the myrtle bowers of bliss
The warrior may remain; he may not see
His laurels pine in shade, or the deep stain
Of rust upon his sword. Again the sound
Of arms recall'd Orlando to the field;
And he will go: not Adelaide's, the love
That would enchain him to its witchery—
No; she would bid her lover from her arms,
E'en tho' her heart were breaking; point to fame,
Albeit 'twere more than death unto her soul!

VIII.

They wander'd thro' a scene, where every spot
Was trac'd with some soft record of the heart;
Where the eye could not glance, but it must gaze
On some memorial of their happiness.
Here wing'd with pleasure moments fled, as in
A magic circle, where hours past, but left
No sorrow for their loss—perish'd like flowers
Dying in odours, while fresh blooms succeed:
But these were dreams of blessedness departed;
And the long lingering looks they now were giving,
Perchance would be their last. Another day,
And, Adelaide, thy love will be afar.
The arm now round thee thrown so tenderly,
Will be the reddest in the ranks of death;
That voice, that sinks so sweetly on thy ear,

Low murmuring the gentle tones of love,
Will swell the war cry, and breathe loud defiance!

IX.

It was a night of summer's mildest reign—
Calm, lonely sweetness! scarce the breeze had pow'r
To waft the fragrant sighs born with the dew;
It did not stir a leaf, nor wake a sound;
But all was quiet as an infant's sleep,
Save when the distant waterfall was heard,
Like airy notes of fairy minstrelsy.
'Twas a fair scene! beside them flowers bloom'd
Such as the earth puts forth to grace the step
Of a celestial visitant: the turf
Gleam'd with the diamond dew; and over head,
The half-form'd crescent of the young moon smil'd
On the blue ocean of the starry heaven;
A few light clouds were wandering around,

Still varying like love's dear uncertainty!
Now flowing gracefully, like beauty's veil,
Now as the frothing waves upon the sea,
And ever, as like snow they scatter'd round,
Gleam'd forth the glorious stars. At distance seen,
The ice-clad mountains rose magnificent,
Like marble palaces that Rome once rear'd
In her now long-past days of mightiness.
Girdling them in dark woods the black pines waved;
O'er them the night had thrown her deepest shroud;
Gloom, where the moon had wasted her sweet smiles;
Shades that she might not pierce, where brightness fell
Vainly, as soothing words upon despair.

X.

They linger'd there, Orlando and his love,
His fair betrothed bride; each step was link'd

With some associate sweetness, and recall'd
Some thought that love had hallow'd. Love will
    shed
His magic hues, where'er his pinions find
A resting place; the wilderness will smile,
And blossom like a rose, if he be there.
They reach'd a shadowy alcove, where oft
Th' unconscious hours had past unmark'd away.
It was in young affection's earliest day
They rais'd the fragrant temple, and then said—
No flower should ever deck their fav'rite haunt,
That was not hallow'd by the minstrel's song,
Or fancy could not paint some tender thought.
They rear'd it 'neath a pine which long had braved
The perilous bursting of the winter's storm;
The stem was yet unbent, but it was scath'd
By the red lightning; and the tempest's wing
Had past it, withering like adversity:
A white rose gracefully around it twin'd,

Cheering its ruin, and united still
Even amid decay, like faithful love,
Clinging more closely to the wounded spirit.
Around were brightest flowers; the myrtle flung
Its snowy buds—a wreath for constancy;
The young moss-rose threw from its vermil cheek,
The green veil, fresh and beautiful as those
That caught their warm carnation from the lips
Of Venus, when she kiss'd their fragrant leaves;
Fraught with cerulean hues, the violet
Half-open'd, timidly, its fair blue eyes;
Close by it's side, the lily pensively
Bow'd down its languid head, pale as the cheek
Faded by sorrow. There the hyacinth bloom'd
With liveliest colours; some like rubies glow'd,
Some bright with tyrian purple; others wore
The melting azure of a summer sky;
Some white and stainless, others ting'd with red,
Like the last warmth of a departing blush.——

Here had they come to watch the earliest smile
Of morning dimple into roseate light;
Here breezes, which had bath'd their burning wings
In streams, whose birth-place is amid the clouds,
Breath'd mountain freshness o'er the sultry noon;
Eve found them here listing her vesper song,
And stars had been the lamps to light their bowers.
And oft at that sweet solitary time
Would young Orlando listen to the voice
Of her he lov'd, soft as the moonlight song
The fabled Syren breath'd; and at his praise
A blush like day-break, and a smile, would play
Upon her cheek—the heart's own eloquence.

XI.

It was the hour of parting, and they breath'd
Those vows of tender constancy,—the hopes,
The fears, the fond regrets that crowd the time

Of love's farewell.   Hope, for what joy can thrill
The maiden's bosom with such throb of bliss,
As when, returning from the fields of death,
The warrior comes in all the pride of fame,
And seeks his dearest trophy in her smile!
Fear, for what heart but sickens at the thought
Of danger darkening round some cherish'd being!
A few short hurried vows of changeless faith,
And their farewell was taken silently.
That sorrow is not much, which seeks for words
To image forth its grief.   Methinks adieu
Is cold, when uttered with aught else but tears.

XII.

'Tis the bright hour of noon; the sun looks forth
In all his splendour, o'er the stirring scene
Of thousands rushing onward to the strife.
They come in armed ranks, and spear and shield

Are glistening in the ray. How beautiful,
How glorious, and how glad they move to death!
The very banners sweep as they were proud
To spread their crimson foldings to the air.
Here the young warrior curbs his foaming steed,
Impatient for his first of fields; and here
The toil-worn veteran, with his locks of age,
White as the war-plume waving o'er his helm,
Pants for the bursting of the battle storm.——
How bright, how envied, is the warrior's fate!
For him will glory bind her choicest wreaths
Of fadeless laurels;—his the stormy joy,
Which the brave spirit feels at honour's call,
When the bard wakes his proudest minstrelsy:
(And what can thrill the harp like warlike theme?)
His deeds will be remembered, and his name
Will live for ever in the breath of song:
Love's fairest roses 'neath the laurel grow,
And woman's fondest sigh is for the brave.

XIII.

Upon a lofty tower stood Adelaide,
And watch'd the scene below: you might have
    gaz'd
On those fair tresses floating in the wind;
The white veil flowing o'er her graceful form,
Her arms cross'd pensively upon her breast,
And eyes, now upwards rais'd in tears to heav'n,
Now glancing mournfully on those beneath,
And deem'd that Peace had paus'd one moment, ere
She wing'd her flight from earth; so fair she was,
Like to some lovely creature of the skies.
Her eye dwelt on Orlando's form, who yet
Linger'd to catch one dear, one parting glance—
That last look, treasur'd so in after hours.
He wore the colours she had given, white
And green, the hue of promise, borne by spring.

He passed, and Adelaide is left with nought
But hope, to cheer away the slow wing'd days.
Hope, frail but lovely shadow ! thou dost come,
Like a bright vision on our pathway here,
Making the gloomy future beautiful,
And gilding our horizon with a light,
The fairest human eye can ever know.
Fav'rite of heaven ! 'twas thine to pledge the cup
Of pleasure's sparkling waters undefil'd ;
But, oh ! the draught was fleeting ! scarce thy lip
Touch'd the clear nectar ere 'twas vanished.
The soul of youth confides in thee ; thy voice
Is love's own halcyon music ; it is thine
To colour every dream of happiness.
I've pictur'd thine a soft etherial form,
Like to some light creation of the clouds—
Some bright aerial wonder ; o'er thy cheek
The rose has shed its beauty ; on thy brow
The golden clusters play enwreath'd with flowers,

Gay with a thousand transitory hues;
The rainbow tints are gleaming in thy wings;
Thy laughing eyes are blue—not the deep shade
Worn by the melancholy violet,
But the clear sunny blue of summer skies;
And in thy hand a glass, wherein the eye
May gaze on many a wonder—all is there
That heart can pant for; many a glorious dream
Meets the rapt sight, no sooner seen than gone.
False as thou art, O most illusive Hope!
Reproach is not for thee : what, tho' the flowers
Which thou dost scatter o'er our pilgrimage,
Are evanescent, yet they are most sweet.
Who would not revel in thy witchery,
Tho' all too soon the spell will be dissolved!
The moments of thy reign are bless'd indeed;
They are the purest pleasures life can boast—
Reality is sadness.———

> But thy power
Sheds its most soothing influence when the heart,
Too full for utterance, beats a fond farewell!
Then beams thy sunshine, lighting up a sky,
Which else were thickest darkness;—for what gloom
Is like the gloom of absence! But for thee,
And thy sweet promises of meeting joys,
The warm embrace, the look of love, the smile,
The blissful words of welcome once again,—
Parting were as the shadow of the grave.

XIV.

Thus far my song hath reach'd again to thee,
With whom my strain began: say, will thy smile
Beam on my harp, like sunshine upon flowers,
Depriv'd of which they die? Oh! if one note

Can boast of sweetness, 'tis from thee 'twas caught.
Enough, enough! whate'er my fate may be,
That song is transport, that wins praise from thee.

CANTO II.

CANTO II.

Once more my harp awakens; once again,
Tho' all unworthy be my hand to twine
Th' etherial blossomings of poetry,
I would call forth its numbers, yet would feel
Its music fall like sunlight on my soul.
Oh, lovely phantom! tho' they say that thou
Art but a light to lead my steps aside;
That thy romance is but a wayward dream;
That few are thy true votaries, and they
Drain to the dregs the cup of bitterness;

And speak in mockery of the glorious wreath,
Whose holiest resting place is in the grave;
Tell of the cold contempt that ever waits
On those who call on thee, and call in vain.—
All this I know and feel, most deeply feel,
How few the favour'd ones on whom thou breathest
The heart's aroma, immortality.
Yet still I love thee, passionately love!
Yet would I dwell on thy fair picturings,
Although thy brightest hues may be no more
Than tulip tints, that colour but to fade.
Sweet Spirit of the Harp! thou canst create
An airy world of beauty and delight,
Far from the chill realities of life,
Where sorrow closely follows pleasure's steps;
Rapture, companion of thy wanderings!
Still, thou enchanting power, my love is thine.—
But yet there is a dearer bliss, than dwells
E'en in these fond illusions;—ah! canst thou,

From whom it came, paint the deep joy, or tell
What the young minstrel feels, when first the song
Has been rewarded by the thrilling praise
Of one too partial, but whose lightest word
Can bid the heart beat quick with happiness—
Recall thine earliest and thy dearest wish—
Recall the first bright vision of thy youth,
The hope, which was, ah! more than life to thee!
Where blended timid fear, whate'er it was
That thy young spirit priz'd, and thou mayst tell,
Were mine the fairest laurel Bard e'er gain'd,
In days when Greece was proud to grace the lyre;
Were mine the fame, before whose glory life
Sinks into nothingness, they could not be
So precious as the slightest wreath of thine:
It is my thought of pride, my cherish'd prize,
To breathe one song not quite unworthy thee.
But, Hope! thy charmed voice I may not trust;
To list to thy sweet promises, is but

To throw the seeds of pleasure to the wind.
What can I look upon but vivid dreams,
That sprang like flowers, and like flowers perish'd
Leaving no trace, save a few whither'd leaves
Trodden to earth, and mouldering round the stem.
Alas! each sunny vision I have known,
Has pass'd away like to an infant's smile—
Bathed the next moment in the bitterest tears.
And shall I raise my hall of joy again,
My fairy dwelling, on th' unstable sand?
With tremulous hand, I scarce dare wake the
      strings;
They too may tell the vanity of hope.

II.

Morn came in joy, and eve in tenderness;
Still Adelaide was lonely in her bower,

While on Orlando hung her every thought.
She sang the songs which once he had call'd sweet,
Cherish'd his favorite flowers, and oft would trace
The haunts his step had sought, and pour'd her soul
In faithful orisons for him to heaven.——
Love for the absent, is as love that dwells
O'er the remembrance of the cherish'd dead;
The same deep feeling—kind, affectionate;
A veil thrown o'er each fault, a purer light
Around each virtue; now like relics priz'd;
'Tis the same feeling, save we do not mourn
With sorrow that can never solace know—
Save that we look with soothing confidence
To the blest moment, when we meet once more!
How we do love the absent! absence is
The moonlight of affection; then the heart,
Sheds o'er each thought a visionary charm,
A chastened pensive beauty; and the shade

That hangs around, like dim futurity,
Tho' the eye may not pierce it, yet it may
Image ideal loveliness, and trace
Bright shapes, which if the shadows were dispell'd,
Might be but blanks; for never yet did life
Present the path of pleasantness we dream'd;
Tho' like the assurance the sweet moonlight gives
Of the reflected sun, our hopes shine forth,
And tell us all that fancy paints is true.

III.

She knelt before the altar, while around
Swell'd deep, slow, solemn music. She was robed,
As a young bride, in rich and rare attire:
The brilliants flash'd, amid the auburn waves
Of her luxuriant hair, and rosy wreathes
Fell with the glossy curls upon her neck.

And bright the sparkling zone round her slight waist,
Fastening the foldings of her snowy robe.—
She knelt, and hid her face; and when she rose,
Her cheek was pale, and bore the trace of tears,
Wearing that look of faded loveliness
Which tells the blight of misery hath pass'd,
And that the heart is withering silently!
She gaz'd upon the glass which stood beside—
It gave a lovely semblance back; a form
Of matchless grace; a face where beauty dwelt;
But sorrow's records there were deeply trac'd.
The eloquence of that soft countenance
Bore the dark characters of grief; the look
She wildly gave, seem'd agony; the tears
That did but tremble 'neath the eyelash, fell
Upon the delicate hand that press'd her brow.
Well might that glance be agony; so fair,
In life's most happy season! yet to her

The future was a blank, the past despair!
She had long loved but too devotedly;—
The dream was over, and she shrank away
From the now joyless world : he who had been
To her the light, the breath of life, was gone.
Memory to her was as a faded flower,
Whose lingering fragrance just recalls how sweet,
How beautiful it has been, but to keep
Regret alive, and make its wither'd state—
More wither'd from its former loveliness.

IV.

They laid aside her gems and costly vest,
And robed her in the simple garb of black.
And those fair tresses, braided o'er her brow
Like golden clusters round pure ivory,
Bright as the locks the Egyptian queen once gave—
A tender offering, worthy her and love—

Were sever'd from her head; and then they threw
The eternal veil upon her face.   Yet still
She seem'd scarce conscious of the scene around:
Even that irrevocable vow, which breaks
All earthly ties, call'd no emotion forth;
Her soul held but one feeling, desolate,
The recklessness of cold and fix'd despair.
The anthem ceas'd, the long last vow is said,
And she is lost for ever to the world!
Many a look on that sweet votary dwelt,
Marvelling that one, in youth's enchanted hour,
Should turn away from life, when life's so fair
As it does ever seem at morning's rise;
When fancy's fairy pencil tints the scene,
Where the warm eye of expectation roves,
Led on by hope, whose wild and gladsome light
Is as a meteor glancing over all;—
At this joy-breathing moment, turn away,
And bid the opening rosebud pine in shade.

Vain idle wonder ! little do they know
How recklessly the eye of sorrow dwells
On youth and loveliness ! What charm has life
To her whose spirit sinks in one deep thought,
One feeling, where all others are absorb'd ;
One lone grief, like the deadly plant which grows
And spreads its venom'd leaves, until around
Nought but a noxious poison'd spot is left,
Where blossoms, fruit, nor even weeds appear;
All lost in that one baleful influence.——
Such, Adelaide, thy fate, e'en in thy morn !
Thy summer-day, when all seem'd fair around,
The desolating pow'r was hov'ring near ;
And the sweet altar, where love's pure light shone,
Was levell'd with the dust ; while the fond heart,
That had uprear'd it, sunk beneath the shock !

V.

She who doth bend her o'er her lover's urn,
And pour the hopeless tears that wail the dead;
Tho' deep, tho' wild her misery may be,
Grief has for her a gentle anodyne.
There is a flower blooms upon the grave,
A life spring, even in the desert found,
A sunny ray upon the vale of tears—
The memory of his faithfulness; the bliss,
That his last thought was her's; that her's the name
That trembled, even in death, upon his lips.
But where's the balm to soothe the heart that pines
'Neath love's unkindness? where's the spell can charm
Sorrow like that away? Who could have dream'd,
A bud so fair would bring such bitter fruit?

VI.

And where was he, Orlando? where was he,
When Adelaide breathed vows, which should have
    been
His own? He stood before the altar too,
And by his side there was a youthful fair;
She was most beautiful, the island queen,
For whose dear love the Grecian wanderer sigh'd,
When on him smil'd the daughter of the sun,
And proffer'd immortality was not
More perfect in her loveliness, as o'er
Her vermil cheek she drew the bridal veil,
To hide the rose-light blush's soft consent.
She was most beautiful; but the black hair,
Like raven plumage on the polish'd front;
The ebon arch, pencill'd so gracefully;
And the dark splendour of those glancing eyes,
Meltingly bright, like to her native heaven

When the night comes, in moonlight and in stars,
Told that she was the child of eastern climes.

VII.

The sultry noon had pass'd, the fresh'ning flowers
Rais'd their declined heads, while the cool gale
Left on each leaf a dewy kiss, and bore
Their perfum'd souls away; the rose, which hid
All day her cheek of fragrance from the sun,
In the protecting shadow of the palm,
Now gave rich offerings forth. There was no
    sound
To break the beauty of eve's light repose,
Save when the fountain threw its sparkling foam
And silver waters o'er the marble floor,
So soft it fell, like music; or the boughs
Whisper'd together yet more softly still.
And when the young Zoraide awoke her lute,

Fit answer to an evening fair as this,
It look'd like fairy land; and she who lean'd .
Beside the fount, whose azure mirror gave
A fresh existence to her loveliness,
Seemed one of those etherial forms, the flowers,
In the wild magic of Arabian tale.
I may not name Arabia, and not pay
The slight meed of my homage to its songs:
How oft I've linger'd o'er the page, which told
Of him, the wand'rer of the sea, and all
The marvels he beheld! and when Gulnare
Unveil'd the glories of the ocean depth,
Or where the Persian and his ill-starr'd love,
United in the grave, found sweet repose!
And him, the Fortunate, whose gorgeous hall
Kings could not match—Aladdin, who possest
The mystic lamp; alas! that days like these,
Of fairy wonders, now should be no more.
How have I shudder'd, when the warning voice

Pass'd o'er the careless city, but in vain!
When the dread curse came down, and one alone
Liv'd (fearful life!) in the sad solitude.
I've hung on the strange witchery, till I've deem'd
The bright creations visible, and seen
Th' enchanted palaces before me rise:
A few brief moments, and how chang'd the scene!
The song is broken off, the shatter'd lute
Spends its last breath in dying murmurings,
Lost in the clang of arms; the fountain wave
Is red with gore, its crystal beauty gone;
And flowers, trodden on the blood-stain'd earth,
Shed their last odorous sigh upon the dead;
While she, their fairy mistress, captive now,
Is pale and senseless in yon warrior's arm!

VIII.

The hour of fear is over, and Zoraide
Has listened to the Christian warrior's tale,
And her young heart is won. Came there no
    thought
Of shame and sorrow, false one, when thy lip
Proffer'd again the vows of changeless faith?
Alas! alas! too often conscience sleeps,
When pleasure's syren numbers lull its rest.—
Oh, Love! when, as thy birthright, there was giv'n
To thee each fairest, each endearing gift,
What demon came, and hid amid thy wreath
The heart-consuming worm, Inconstancy?
'Tis well; for were thy blissfulness less fleet,
It were a joy to render life too dear,
Whoe'er could brook to leave their earthly home,
If it were love's unchangeable abode?

There are some moments in our path of life,
Like showers mid drought, or sunshine amid
    showers,
Awakening every feeling of delight
With which the soul can thrill in rapturous joy.
Such is the warrior's happiness, when, come
From the dark fields of death, he sees once more
The treasures lost so long, now found again;
Sees gladness in each face, and hears the words
Of heart-breathed welcome, from each lip he loves;
When the dim eye of age again grows bright
To look upon him; and within his arms
Reclines the cherish'd one, whose tender smile,
And soft eyes melting with delicious tears,
Eagerly dwell on the dear stranger's face.—
Happiness, soon thy dwelling may be found!
Fly from the heartless pleasures of the world,
Those passing lights, that dazzle to deceive!
Seek that bright spot of blessedness, thy home—

All that this life can give of pure and dear—
Changeless affection, kindness still the same,
The ear that listens but to soothe thy grief—
That never tedious thinks thy tale of joy;
The look, that shares thy hope and soothes thy fear;
The smile still fondly answering thy own;
Each dream of bliss, and each desire of love,
Is in the magic circle of thy hearth.

X.

Full gallantly Orlando stemm'd the tide,
The stormy tide of battle; he had been
Amid the bravest champions of the Cross!
At length the gloomy night of warfare clos'd,
And the sweet smile of peace dawn'd o'er the sky,
And homeward turn'd the warriors. Italy
First greeted them again; but as they sought
Orlando and his beautiful Zoraide,

His natal towers, it chanc'd their mountain guide
Unheedful wander'd from the purpos'd path
Around the dark wood twined; ages had pass'd
Since those huge trees were saplings of the spring,
And trembled when the slightest breeze pass'd by.
Now they rose giants, in their hour of pride,
Stood in their strength, and braved the blast of
    heaven:
Naked they stood and desolate; the oaks,
Which, garb'd in summer foliage, had been
The glory of the forest, worn and bare,
Were now like monuments of time's decay;
The leaves were gone from all, save where the pine
Threw the wide shadow of its unchang'd green.
I could not envy it that fadeless state.—
Ah! who would be the last, the only one
That ruin spares—no; if the blight must pass
O'er all around, let it pass o'er me too!——
The moon was darken'd by a clouded heaven;

No sweets, no music, rose to welcome her;
The birds did seem to dread such solitude:
Nor flowers could spring upon that dank cold
    earth.
Fierce o'er the snowy mountains swept the wind,
With wild lament; it seem'd the unearthly wail
Of unforgiven souls, or as the yell
Of evil spirits riding on the gale.——
They gain'd an opener space; at distance seen,
Uprose a lighted tower; and where's the chief
Would not throw wide the hospitable gate,
And gladly hail the swords of Palestine?
Free was the welcome, fairly spread the feast;
Proudly the host receiv'd his honour'd guest:
But chill the damp upon Orlando's heart—
Was it a dream!—he stood in Ethlin's hall!

XI.

The wine cup circles; thro' the festal train
The sound of mirth and revelry is heard;
The minstrels strike the harp, and proudly raise
The song of triumph; round the cheerful board
Are gallant warriors! many a one is there,
Whose fame were fitting theme for minstrel song.
But turn we from these flowers of chivalry,
To yonder chief, who leans abstractedly,
As if some shadow on his spirit hung;
Some dreaming mood, that comes when present scenes
Recall long absent thoughts, and bring to mind
What yet would be most willingly forgotten.
Orlando! there is gloom upon thy brow!
Can Ethlin's be a hall of joy to thee?

Beside thee sits thy young and lovely bride—
Who does not envy thee so fair a prize;
The bard is telling of thy glorious deeds,
And many a lady's eye is bent on thee.
The voice of pleasure is not heard; in vain
The goblet sparkles, and the song is breathed;
Even beauty's smile glanced unregarded by!
Came not the days long past upon thy soul,
Weighing the spirit down, like fearful forms,
The dreary shapes that crowd a fever'd dream?
He thought on Adelaide;—oh! where was she?
Her place was vacant, and all seemed so strange!
She was the last fair scion of her race;
The lofty pillars of proud Ethlin's line
Were broken all; and now another lord
Bore sway, in that too well remember'd hall.
They spoke of him, the late chief of these towers;
He too had pass'd unto his place of rest.
And then, with kindling cheek, Orlando heard

Yet once again, the name of Adelaide :
They told, a lonely orphan, she had sought
The convent's silent shade : some secret grief
Had prey'd upon her ; and it had been said,
She was a victim at the sacred shrine—
Rather the bride of sorrow than of heaven.
He heard no more, but left the mirthful group,
And sought again the groves, where once young
    love
Had borne the halcyon hours upon his wing,
Roaming in that strange mood, when conscious
    wrong.
Presses upon the heart ;—when feelings rise,
We may not brook another's eye should see ;
When memory haunts us, as a spectred form
On which we dare not gaze, and solitude
Is what we tremble at, yet what we seek.

XII.

'Tis soothing, oh ! most soothing to the heart,
To rove 'mid scenes where once we have been blest!
Each tree, each blossom, has a thrilling charm;
They seem memorials of those happier hours :
The very sigh that tells they are no more,
Is sweet unto the spirit ; former days,
And former feelings, rise upon the soul,
Dear as they once have been.   Again the heart
Throbs warmly, fondly, as 'twas wont to do.
Thou, who art yet with young hopes undecay'd,
With unscath'd happiness, thy bosom guest,
Unchill'd by sorrow; 'tis not thine to tell
How soon the warmth, the purity will fade,
Of thy once lovely wild imaginings !
Thou canst not tell how dear they'll be to thee,

'Mid coming clouds; or how thy thoughts will fear
To catch from the remembrance of the past,
A faint reflection of thy former bliss!
Thine eye is looking now to future hours,
Where hope has traced for thee a fairy land;
Pass but a little while, and thou wilt shrink
From the cold visions of futurity,
Which thou, alas! hast learnt to know too well;
And turn to that dear time, ere sadness threw
Its shadow o'er thy prospect; when thy soul
Shed over all its own romantic light;
Ere falsehood, disappointment, grief, and wrong,
Wither'd the feelings of thy opening youth—
Leaving thee, like the bud the worm hath scath'd,
Bloom on its cheek—the canker in its heart.

XIII.

Orlando rov'd around; not his the bliss
That breathes from recollections like the sigh
Exhaling fragrance from the faded rose.
Ah! how unlike the calm and lovely nights,
When last with Adelaide he wander'd here!
Then the moon glanced upon a summer sky—
A smiling queen amid her starry court—
And all around was loveliness, and love.
Now the departing autumn's shadowy hours
Were passing in their gloom. Dark season! thou
Alone dost give a stern unkind farewell!—
Fair is the young spring, with her golden hair
And braids of dewy flowers, and her brow
Has the soft beauty of a timid girl;
And, like a blushing bride, the summer comes,

While the sun smiles upon his favorite child :
When first thou dost magnificent succeed
To the bright chariot of the circling year,
The valleys laugh, and plenty greets thy steps ;
Around thee then the cheerful cornfields wave,
And purple clusters sparkle on the vine ;
Then the rich tints are colouring the leaves,
Like the pavilion of an eastern king,
And flowers breathe their latest, sweetest sigh.
Soon is thy beauty gone ! the leaves and flowers,
That welcom'd thee at first, are quickly gone,
Like faithless friends that flee adversity ;
Then round thee blow the keen winds, like re-
    proach,
That ever wait upon the sunless day.—
Thy brow is sad, thy sky is lost in clouds,
And darkness is around thee as a robe.
Spring blushes into summer ; summer goes,
And leaves a glorious trace of light behind ;—

E'en winter softens into sunny spring ;—
But thou, pale melancholy season ! thou
Alone departest in thine hour of wrath ?

XIV.

How chang'd the scene from what it once had been!
Now loneliness hung o'er it like a cloud !
The myrtle bower they'd twin'd so gracefully,
No trace of it was left ; and that white rose,
That wreath'd so fondly round the blasted pine,
Was gone—the tree stood now quite desolate.
Beneath, half-hidden by the briars round,
And green with moss, there was a broken harp :
Time had been, when those now so silent chords
Were sweet as hope's soft prophecy of love ;
Now his heart died within him, as the breeze
Waked, faintly wak'd, the few remaining strings.

He turn'd him from the grove, where each thing
	was
A witness of the sorrow he had caus'd;
Yet still he wander'd on: at length his step
Paus'd 'mid the silent dwellings of the dead.
Here where the yew, dark emblem of despair!
Threw its black shadow, Ethlin's race repos'd.
Here lay the vet'ran—his long warfare o'er;
The youthful hero, fallen like the pine
In its first summer; and the maiden's tomb,
Whose beauty was but as a fairy dream.

XV.

There was one grave—he knew it well again,
For he had often knelt with Adelaide,
When the affectionate tribute of her tears
Were offer'd to the dead;—what was that voice

Waking the silent night ? he look'd around :
A maiden, by her dark veil half conceal'd,
Was leaning on the tomb, breathing low sounds,
Like grief's low accents wailing o'er the sod.
He gaz'd upon her—it was Adelaide !——
In the wild dream of phrenzy, she had fled
Her convent's cell, and sought her brother's urn:
She sank on the cold turf! the moonlight fell
Upon her pallid face.—Alas ! how chang'd
From the fair rose he left ! Her faded cheek
Wore a strange ghastly hue ; her eye was dim—
Ah ! how unlike its once so lovely light !—
Half clos'd and rayless ; and the drooping lash
Hung heavily upon the glossy blue :
Her form was wasted, and her gasping lip
Had lost its rosy beauty ; she was now
But the last shade of blighted loveliness !——
He knelt beside her, but she knew him not—
The chill of death was freezing round her heart;

Her hand was ice, the life pulse was unheard;
But at his passionate and wild lament,
A ray yet glanc'd upon her vacant eye,
Which to Orlando turn'd, as it would close
In gazing on the face she had so lov'd;—
Then faintly strove to breathe forgiving sounds,
Low, inarticulate. Upon her neck
He threw himself;—that murmur was her last—
The lip he press'd was cold!

XVI.

A curse was laid upon him!—gold and power,
Beauty and fame were his, yet still there hung
That shadow on his brow; and never smile
Was seen to lighten o'er his face: he mov'd
As if beneath the influence of some spell,
Darkening his soul; his sleep was not repose.

Then wild creations haunted him, and shapes
Of terror and of evil; and a form,
A wan and wasted form, rose on his dreams,
Till rest was agony! There was a fire,
By day and night, consuming at his heart;
A withering seal was set on every thought—
All ministers of bitterness; he shunn'd
The haunts of pleasure; still that dying look
Of sweet forgiveness, and the last faint tone
Of her he had deserted, tortur'd him.

XVII.

She mark'd the change (his fair Zoraide), and strove,
With all a woman's winning tenderness,
To soothe his gloomy spirit, but in vain—
The shadow of his soul fell o'er her too:

Her cheek grew pale with frequent tears, that wore
The rose away. Oh! burning are the drops
That wounded love will shed—like to the dew
Falling from off the poison tree, the blight
Still following the touch;—ah! other tears
Soften and bless—but these destroy the heart.
She was alone, a stranger in the land;
All her hopes dwelt upon him; she was as
A sunborn flower of her native plains,
Borne to far northern climes; it languishes
When its bright lover, the all-glorious sun,
That erst looked smiling on its beauty, turns
A cold and clouded glance—its drooping head
Sickens and pines. Thus fared it with Zoraide—
Passing as flits a morning dream away.

XVIII.

What was his life thenceforth?—a fiery page,

Traced with unreal characters; a night
Gleaming with meteor flashes. They had laid
Zoraide (for thus she wish'd it) by the side
Of her sweet rival: there he leant:—morn came,
And found him bending there; the evening dew
Fell damp upon his brow; his sole employ
To braid these graves with fairest blossomings,
While visions wild, and fearful images
Of woe—the relics of reality—
Usurp'd the throne of the etherial mind:
This might not be for long. When first he twin'd
His offerings round those tombs, the bee had just
Wak'd his soft music in the violet;
And when the autumn's amber clusters shone
Upon the green leav'd vines, Orlando slept
In the dark shadowy dwellings of the dead!

MISCELLANEOUS POEMS.

THE FAREWELL.

Farewell! companion of my solitude!
Light of my loneliness, my heart's desire;
Spirit, that wander'd o'er the soft harp's strings,
Farewell! awhile I wake me from thy dream;
Fondly farewell, adored one! to thee.——
Rose of my soul! beside the social hearth
Was thy first springing up; thy ev'ry shoot
Was brighten'd in the smile of those most dear:
Affection was thy sunlight and thy dew.
And when thy bloom was lonely, when no more
The eyes I lov'd watch'd o'er thy growth, thou wert
The blest memorial of those far away—
Thy blossoms breath'd of happiness and home.

What joy to think, perchance some future day,
Those looks would dwell on thee again, and greet
The buds expanding, and thy new sprung leaves!
Thou, Poetry, in absence wert a chain,
Binding our hearts together: where so well
As in thy numbers, could I pour my soul,
In soothing tenderness? 'twas bliss, to make
Thought visible to those of whom I thought.
Now that enchantment over, thy slight bark
Adventures in a wide and perilous sea;
Dark are the waves around thy fragile skiff;
Unskilful is the hand which pilots thee;
And few have ever reach'd thy destin'd shore.
I part from thee, as I should part from one
Whom I may wish, not hope, to see again.
Fondly, and fearfully, farewell to thee,
Sweet sojourner, so long my bosom guest!
Perhaps a long, perhaps a last farewell!

LINES TO ———

Think of me, and I'll tell thee when
    The moment of that thought shall be;
When yon sweet star is rising, then,
    Oh! then, beloved! think of me.
Ah! let thy mem'ry on me rest,
    When, pale and beautiful as now,
Yon planet sinks beneath the west
    With dewy light and silver brow.

When the blue arch of heaven is bright,
    When not a shadow frowns above,

The beauty of its placid light
  Will seem the emblem of our love.
When clouds are gathering on its way,
  And the black storms around it wait,
The darkness of its shrouded ray
  Will seem the emblem of our fate.

FRAGMENT.

Love thee! yes, yes! the storms that rend aside
All other ties will but entwine my heart
More closely, more devotedly to thine.
Love thee!—but that I know how heavily
Sorrow hath press'd thy generous spirit down,
I should almost reproach thee for the doubt!
I have no thought, that does not dwell on thee;
No hope, in which thou minglest not; no wish,
In which thou bearest no part; my orisons
To heaven, begin and end with thy dear name:
My fate is link'd with thine—I did not plight

My vows to thee for a mere summer day,
But still to be unchang'd; it was most sweet
To share thy sunlight of prosperity,
Thine hours of brightness; now I only ask
To share thy sorrow, and to be to thee
All tenderness, and love, and constancy—
A feeling, lighting up thy desolate heart;
A fountain springing in the wilderness;
Or as the breeze upon the fever'd brow,
Soothing the pain it may not chase away.

ABSENCE.

"Cesser d'exister n'est rien, se quitter est le plus grand des maux."

"And all the fix'd delights of house and home—
Friendship that cannot break, and love that will not
    roam."

I will not say, I fear your absent one
Will be forgotten; but you cannot feel
The darkening thoughts that o'er my spirits steal,
When I remember I am quite alone—
That all I lov'd most fondly, all are gone.
To you that deepest sorrow is unknown:

Some very dear ones are beside you now;
But cold is here each smile that meets my own;
It does not lighten o'er some long lov'd brow.
'Tis vain to tell me soon again we meet—
That thought but makes the weary hours depart
More slowly : hope is sickness to the heart.
When we so oft its accents must repeat.
Affection is, in absence, as the flower
Transplanted from the soil which gave it birth—
Dew has no freshness, sunshine has no power;
Drooping, it pines for its lov'd native earth.

CURTIUS.

There is a multitude, in number like
The waves of the wide ocean; and as still
As are those waters, when the summer breeze
Sleeps on the moveless billow; there is awe
On every countenance; and each does stand
In gasping breathlessness, as terror chain'd
The life pulse down; or, as they deem'd, a sound
Might call down new destruction on their heads.—
The sun look'd smiling from his clear blue throne,
And nature seem'd to gladden in the ray;
When suddenly a cloud came over heaven,

A black and terrible shadow, as the gloom
Of the destroying angel's form; the wind
Swept past with hollow murmur; and the birds
Ceasing their song of joyfulness, with mute,
And quick, and tremulous flight, for shelter sought!
Fear was on every living thing : the earth
Trembled as she presag'd some coming ill;
The voice of thunder spake; and in the midst
Of that proud city, in the midst of Rome,
The ground was riven in twain; and in the spot,
Where human steps had but so lately been,
There yawn'd a fearful gulf, dark as the powers
Of hell were gather'd there—no eye might scan
That fathomless abyss; the augur's voice
Hath told the will of heaven—nought may close
That gulf of terror, till it is the grave
Of all Rome holds most precious. Then came forth
A youthful warrior—" What is dear to Rome,
But patriot valour? Ye infernal Gods,

Who now look wrathful from your deep abodes,
Behold your ready sacrifice!" He comes,
Arm'd as for battle, save no plumed helm
His black hair presses: he is on the steed
Which has so often borne him to the field.—
Young Curtius came, but with a brow as firm,
And cheek unchang'd, as he was wont to wear,
When he essay'd the glorious strife of men;
Pride glanced upon his eye—but pride that seem'd
As a remembrance of the higher state
In which aspiring spirits move; whose thoughts
Of avarice, indolence, and selfish care,
The chains of meaner ones, have given way
Before the mighty fire of the high soul—
Whose hope is immortality, whose steps
Are steps of flame, on which the many gaze,
But dare not follow. He one moment paus'd,
And cast a farewell look on all around.
How beautiful must be the sky above,

And fair the earth beneath, to him who gives
A lingering look, and knows it is his last!—
Then onward urg'd his courser.——Hark! a voice,
A wild shriek rings upon the air: he turn'd,
And his glance fell on her, his own dear love.
She rush'd upon his bosom silently,
As if her life were in that last embrace.
All was so still around, that every sob,
And the heart's throb of agony, were heard.
He clasp'd her, without power to soothe her grief,
But press'd her coral lip—did never flower
Yield fresher incense forth!—and kiss'd away
The tears on her pale cheek, then on her gaz'd.—
All his deep feeling, anguish, high resolves,
And love intense, were in that passionate glance.
He clasp'd her wildly, and his dark eye swam
In tenderness; but he has nerv'd his soul—
He has spurr'd on—and the dread gulf is clos'd!

Sketch of a Painting of Santa Malvidera, escaped miraculously from Shipwreck.

She knelt upon the rock; her graceful arms
Were rais'd to heaven, in attitude of prayer:
You might have gaz'd on those half-opened lips,
And deem'd you listen'd to their silvery tones.
Sweet tears were trembling in her fair blue eyes,
Like drops that linger on the violet—
The glistening relics of a summer shower:
They were the tears of pious gratitude;
And hope, like sunshine, brighten'd thro' their dew.
She look'd all stainless purity; her glance

Spoke of unearthly things, and of a soul
Already mingled with its native skies :
She knelt on the cold rock, while the rude waves
Dash'd o'er her slender form their foam ; around
Was a drear solitude, where the dark cliffs
Frown'd o'er the sea; and the black shadowy clouds,
Gathering their sullen masses, seem'd to be
The tempests' dwelling place. Yet that young saint
Pray'd fearlessly; she felt, the guardian hand,
So late stretch'd forth to save in peril's hour,
Would not desert her now.

SONNET.

Green willow! over whom the perilous blast
Is sweeping roughly; thou dost seem to me
The patient image of humility,
Waiting in meekness till the storm be pass'd,
Assured an hour of peace will come at last;
That there will be for thee a calm bright day,
When the dark clouds are gathered away.
How canst thou ever sorrow's emblem be?
Rather I deem thy slight and fragile form,
In mild endurance bending gracefully,
Is like the wounded heart, which, 'mid the storm,
Looks for the promis'd time which is to be,
In pious confidence. Thou shouldest wave
Thy branches o'er the lowly martyr's grave.

SONNET.

It is not in the day of revelry,
When that the cup of joy is bright and sweet,
And the fresh blossoms spring beneath our feet,
That we reflect on that, where yet must be
Our rock of hope and trust—eternity.
But let the weeds of care, the thorns of strife,
Rise in their darkness o'er our path of life;
Then the pale mourner looks beyond the tomb.
There are some flowers, whose breathings of perfume
Are shed in the night season; so the heart
Yields forth the fragrance of its better part,
When sinks its summer sunlight into gloom:
Most holy in the shadowy hour is given
The soul's best incense, which springs up to heaven

STANZAS.

I do not weep that thou art laid
Within the silent tomb;
I weep not that the cold death-shade
Hath marr'd thy youth's sweet bloom.
'Tis with no wish to wake thy sleep
These tears thy grave bedew;
Ah, no!—ah, no! I only weep
I am not sleeping too.
What is my life, but a vain show,
Of its last hope bereft?
What spell can soothe the soul of woe,
That has but memory left?
How dear, how very dear thou art,
These bitter drops may tell;—
Sole treasure of my lonely heart,
A long and sad farewell!

THE VILLAGE OF THE LEPERS.

[Taken from the Account in the Literary Gazette.]

There was a curse on the unhappy race—
They dwelt apart from all their fellow men—
Sad weary solitude! and every eye
Was turn'd away in loathing. I did pass
Thro' their lone village: silence brooded round,
And misery had set her withering stamp
On every brow; rayless and dim each eye,
And a wan sickly hue was on each face:
They had a look of hopeless wretchedness.
To them the voice of kindness was a sound

Unheard, unwish'd for; no one came to soothe
Their days of bitterness; proscribed, and left
Alone, to struggle with despair and pain :
Riven asunder all the blessed ties
Which are the hope and happiness of life;
Polluted, desolate, the cup of wrath
Had pour'd its utmost fury on their heads.
And there was one, whose image long hath dwelt,
Like to a thought of sorrow on my soul :
She had been beautiful, but now her cheek
Was deadly pale; and from her parched lip
The rose had fled, and left it colourless;
And in her eye, one same expression dwelt,
Of heartless, comfortless despondency!
Her brow was care-worn, blighted by the scathe
Of fell disease, which had destroy'd her prime,
And wither'd youth, when youth is loveliest.
She turn'd her from my look—the curious gaze,
To sorrow is a piercing mockery.

LINES ON ——

I saw thy cheek when 'twas fresh as spring,
Like a May rose newly blossoming;
When thy lip was red as the coral flower,—
Stainless and pure in the deep sea bower.

I saw thy brow when 'twas gay and fair—
Sorrow had then thrown no shadow there;
It was a sweet, a beautiful throne,
That love himself had been proud to own.

Smiles play'd o'er thy face, like the silvery light
The moon throws over the waters by night;
The halcyon's blue had tinted thine eyes,
Sunny and bright as the summer skies.

Thy laugh was glad as the sky lark's lay,
Thy step was light as the waterfall's spray—
When love and when pleasure around thee were
    glowing,
Like some bright bud in Eden blowing.

But now thou art chang'd! it is sad to gaze
On the faded beauty thy form displays;
Thy cheek is pale as the sickly flower,
Struggling in cold spring's sunless hour.

Thy blush is gone, and thy smile is fled,
And thy wan lip hath lost its delicate red;
Tears dim the light of thine azure eye,
And the dimple is banish'd by misery.

Nought rests of what once was so fair,
But thy glossy curls of auburn hair;
The golden braids seem too bright to twine
O'er a brow so shaded by sadness as thine.

Love has been to thee as the treacherous gale,
Opening the rose's mossy veil;
Sweetly it came, but its breath left there
The canker, Remorse, and the blight, Despair!

FRAGMENT.

It is not spring, but still the new-come year
Bears on its softened brow sweet promises
Of soon returning smiles;—twilight again
Claims her soft reign of one delicious hour;
When the red sunset, fading from above,
Leaves on the west an arch of silvery light—
A fairy garden for the evening star
Ere yet the other glorious lamps of heaven
Look on her vesper solitude; or ere
The moon has risen o'er yon shadowy hills.
The hazel flings its yellow blossomings,

And some green traces of expected May
Are venturing to show forth; tho' not as yet
The violet or primrose have awak'd,
Or the wild rose blush'd faintly into bud;
Only the languid snow-drop now is seen—
A melancholy harbinger of joy,
Whose delicate beauty is but for a day,
To welcome in the spring, and then to die.
And by it is the deadly aconite—
To look upon, a pale and innocent flower—
Alas! that even in this first fair gift,
This early wreath, there should the poison lurk!
But it is thus with every loveliness:
Either so frail, its life is but a breath,
Or else some bitterness grows by its side.

PORTRAIT.

I GAZ'D admiringly upon his face;
Th' etherial fire, that kindles from the heart
Of inspiration, lighted up his brow.
There was a wild expression in his eye,
A brilliancy, a deep impassion'd glance,
Which look'd as it had gaz'd on glorious dreams,
And strange and beautiful imaginings,
Until it had reflected back their splendour,
As it communion held with the young storm,
Rolling its gather'd darkness o'er the sky;
And watch'd the golden palace, which the sun

Uprears at eve, of crimson clouds, and all
The earth's magnificence, until his soul
Grew raptured with the wonders it beheld,
And fill'd his eyes with an unearthly light—
A radiance too intense, but that the veil
Of the dark lash, softened its glowing ray.
It was a glance, that dwells upon the thought,
And bids us look for some excelling being
Fraught with rare gifts of the immortal mind.

TO ———

Oh! say not, that I love not nature's face,
And that I cannot know her beauty's power!
Pleasure is unto me a lonely thing:
Deep sorrow, or rapt joy, I cannot feel,
But in still solitude: I may not brook
Another's eye should mark my secret thoughts.
Since the first hour that tears or smiles were mine,
I never sought communion in my grief,
And none could share my silent happiness.
If thou would'st know how I do love to gaze

On nature's face, spring from thy sleepless couch,
And mark the moonlight, when no one may see
Thy deep emotion, and no idle word
Of heartless praise disturb thy soul-felt spell;
Gaze on the stars, till thou dost deem the gale
That murmurs by is music from the spheres,
No taint of earth upon thy dream of heaven;
Watch the bright farewell of the sun, when he
Seeks the white bosom of his ocean-love.
Look on those glorious tints, till thou dost wish
Thou wert a beautiful shadow like to them—
A transitory, but a brilliant thing,
Born amid glory, past away in light;
Ah! then, indeed, nature has magic charms,
And I do love to dwell upon them then.

CORINNA.

She stood alone; but on her every eye
Dwelt in mute ravishment; her long black hair
Flew loose upon the gale, but half confin'd
By the light veil and wreathes of braided rose,
Shading her bosom's matchless ivory,
And fell upon the lyre, like hyacinths
Twin'd fancifully round; a pensive shade
Was on the brightness of her deep blue eyes,
Where the sweet tenderness of woman's glance
Softened the minstrel's fire that sparkled there.—
The song arose; it was just such a strain

The soft Erato wakes, when she would sing
Of loveliness, and love by sorrow shaded;
Her voice (the Syren's is not sweeter, when
She breathes her music to calm moonlight seas,)
Was fraught with tender feelings, and called forth
An answering harmony within the heart;
And even when it ceas'd, the list'ner's ear,
Thrill'd with its wild and witching melody.
She stood, like some fair creature of the skies,
In mild unconscious beauty, and her eyes
Sunk to their timid station on the ground:
Her cheek was delicately pale; but when
They placed the laurel crown upon her brow,
Her face was mantled by a burning blush,
Bright, beautiful, like summer's glowing eve,
Such as young Psyche wore, when Love first taught
His own sweet language.

SLEEPING CHILD.

How innocent, how beautiful thy sleep!
Sweet one, 'tis peace and joy to gaze on thee!
Thy summer sports, thy cloudless gaiety,
Are hush'd in slumber; but there lingers still
A smile upon thy lips, like the young day,
Flinging its sunlight o'er the half-blown rose;
Thy laughing eyes are clos'd, while the dark lash
Rests on thy dimpled cheek, where health has shed
Its liveliest carnation; unconfin'd,
Like golden clusters, shadowing thy face,
Thy chesnut curls twine round thy little arm,

Half hidden by the violets, which breathe
Their fragrance o'er thy head; thy snowy brow
Is clear and open as a shadeless sky:
There are no records there to tell of griefs,
That came like blights in spring, or winter storms
Of tortured feelings, withering cares and joys,
Whose end was bitterness; but here are found
Pure innocence and love, and happiness.

LINES

ADDRESSED TO COLONEL H——,

ON HIS RETURN FROM WATERLOO.

Who envies not the glory of the brave!
The sunshine of their fame—their laurell'd grave!
Theirs is the memory of afterlight;
Theirs is a brightness 'mid oblivion's night:
Time whelms the many with eternal gloom,
But sheds fresh honours on the heros' tomb.
In life, they move not with the common throng,

To them the nobler heights of fame belong;
Each heart admires, each lip is warm with praise;
Each hand would weave the victor-chieftain's bays.
Warrior, this praise is thine ! but there will be
A purer, holier, dearer mead for thee :
Thine was the arm that stopp'd the destin'd blow,
And spar'd the triumph of a fallen foe.
The wreath that valour's deeds must gain is bright—
But its chief lustre flows from mercy's light.

LOVE's PARTING WREATH.

I GIVE thee, love, a blooming braid;
   I cull'd it at eve's 'witching hour;
I twin'd it in the moon's sweet shade,
   When starlight dew was on each flower.

I chose the myrtle's fadeless leaf,
   For it will picture faith to thee;
I chose the cypress—'tis like grief—
   And that may well my emblem be.

I place the violet in my wreath—
  Its sigh is memory's perfume;
I place the rose, for its sweet breath
  Survives its beauty's passing bloom.

Oh! not a flower is here entwin'd,
  That lays not on thy thought a spell:
Forget-me-not, the wreath shall bind—
  Forget me not, is Love's farewell.

ANSWER.

The wreath you gave me, love, is dead,
The bloom is from the roses fled;
A blight is o'er the myrtle shed,
    The violets are withering.
Ah! who that gaz'd upon them now,
Saw each dry leaf, each faded glow,
    Could deem them worth the gathering!

The vows you breathed me, love, were dear;
They fell like music on my ear,
But left behind a sigh, a tear—
    For they were but deceiving.

And who, that thought upon them now,
Would deem each heartless, broken vow,
  Had e'er been worth believing?

Fond dreams, like summer flowers, fall,
And wither'd leaves and thorns are all
They leave their memory to recall,
  So quickly have they perished;
And love that could so soon depart,
That open'd but to chill the heart,
  Will not be long time cherished.

DIRGE.

Oh, calm be thy slumbers!
The cypress shall wave,
The harp pour its numbers
Of grief o'er thy grave.
I'll scatter each blossom
Upon thy cold stone:
The rose's white bosom,
Pure, fair, as thine own;
The violet glowing,
Blue, like to thine eyes;
The jessamine, throwing
Its sweets, like thy sighs.

Like thee, they'll be gather'd
All fresh in their prime;
Like thee, they'll be wither'd
Before it is time:
The flowers we strew o'er thee,
Will fade like thy bloom;
Like the hearts that adore thee,
They'll die on thy tomb!

SONNET.

I ENVY not the traveller's delight,
When he looks on Italia's loveliness,
Or the Swiss mountains rise before his sight;
The view to me would be but loneliness,
Remembering me that I was far away
(Like to a leaf, borne from its natural spray)
From my own dwelling. It does seem most strange,
What happiness it can be thus to range:
Let others roam this world of wonders through—
Theirs be each beauty of the earth and sea;
The flower gemm'd green, the narrow arch of blue,
Around my home, will be enough for me.
I cannot envy him, whose footsteps rove
At distance from the dear ones of his love.

ABSENCE.

"Song is but the eloquence of truth."
                                    CAMPBELL.

Oh! never can we feel how dear
Each lov'd one is, till we have known
The deep regret, the bitter tear,
That comes when those lov'd ones are gone.
It is not till the flowers are pass'd,
That breath'd on summer's perfum'd air,
Till but in memory they last,

That we can feel how sweet they were:
'Tis only at the parting hour,
Affection claims her thrilling power.

There are a thousand ties that wreathe
Around that word of magic—home;
Cold is the heart that e're could breathe
A wish from that lov'd spot to roam.
How fondly now my thoughts retrace—
All once so priz'd, now still more dear—
Each look of love, each gentle face,
The tender word, the parting tear;
Cherish'd and unforgotten seem
The gems of memory's sweetest dream.

As pants the hart in the long chace
For streams where the cool water flows,
So seeks my soul the resting place,
Where all its thoughts, its wishes close.

So dwells my spirit on the hour,
When we shall meet in joy again;
Hope has enwreath'd full many a flower—
Oh! may her visions not be vain!
The world has not a joy for me,
Dear as our meeting thus would be.

A LOVER's DREAM.

It was a dream, as bright as e'er
   Yet glanc'd upon a sleeper's brain;
For fancy's witching wing was there,
   And love had gilded slumber's chain.

There was an eye, like noontide light,
   A voice, like notes of minstrelsy;
That voice was soft, those eyes were bright,
   For, oh! they breathed of love to me.

114

There was a form of loveliness,
   Whose look of tenderness was mine;
My Katherine, dear, canst thou not guess,
   That form of loveliness was thine?

And smil'st thou at my dream, my love?
   No more a vision let it be;
But bid the dreamer's slumber prove
   An image of reality.

THE PHŒNIX AND THE DOVE.

[The Hint taken from the French of Millevoix.]

My wings are bright with the rainbow's dyes,
   My birth is amid perfume;
My death-song is music's sweetest sighs;
   The sun himself lights my tomb.
My flight is traced in the clouds above;
   The grave teems with life for me;
I stand alone—Alone! cried the dove—
   Oh, I then can but pity thee!

LOVE's CHOICE.

[From the same.]

Too long the daring power of love
Had braved the angry gods above:
His doom is seal'd—the doom of heaven—
Love may not hope to be forgiven.
They took away his bow of gold,
And from his eyes the veil unroll'd;
His rose-wreathed quiver is unbound;
His sparkling darts bestrew the ground.
But Venus wept—can such sweet rain
From beauty's eyes e'er fall in vain?
Jove gaz'd on Cytherea's tear,
And own'd his sentence too severe.
" Well, let the boy one treasure keep;
The one he may most dearly prize,
That let him chuse." Love ceas'd to weep,
And caught the veil that blinds his eyes.

THE STAR.

Oh! would I might share thy wild car,
Thou strange and magnificent star!
Thou scatterest thy fiery hair;
Thy steps they are bright on the air—
Behind thee a glorious light;
Streams o'er the dark bosom of night.
Where hast thou been? is the sun
Thy home, when thy journey is done?
Or art thou a wand'rer on high,
No rest for thee found in the sky?

Never again shall I gaze
On the gleam of thy wonderful rays.
Soon the hour of thy splendour is o'er;
I shall look on thy beauty no more:
Thou wilt pass thro' the infinite space—
No mortal thy pathway may trace.
There is mystery stamp'd on thy brow—
A marvel, a secret, art thou.
Oh! would that to me it were given,
To wander with thee thro' the heav'n.

STANZAS,

ADAPTED TO MUSIC BY ——

My heart is as light as the gossamer veil,
That floats on the bosom of air;
It changes as oft as the varying sail—
Like a butterfly, roams without care.
Love, like a flower, is but fair for awhile;
Its freshness soon passes away;
To-morrow I'll seek in some newly-found smile,
The charm that delights me to day.
That cup may be sweetest which deepest is drunk;
Be it mine but the surface to sip:

When once from the top the bright bubbles have
    sunk,
Oh! then let it pass from my lip!
That love may be blissful, whose roses can bind
For ever the heart to its shrine;
But as well you might chain the light wings of the
    wind,
As throw fetters for long over mine.
Thus gaily I'll rove, o'er the blossoms of love,
Just catching their sweets as I fly;
As the zephyr, that transiently bends from above
A fresh flower for every sigh.

ANSWER TO ——

Twine not the cypress round my harp—
It wears too dull a shade for me;
    Light as the flowers
    Of April bowers,
The wreath that encircles my harp must be.

If you will twine a wreath for me,
Twine it of blooms that vanish soon;
    Let each fair hue
    Be wet with dew,
But dew that will pass in the smile of noon.

Light is the spirit of my harp—
  'Twas love and hope first wak'd its strain;
    Awhile sorrow's wings
    May o'ershadow the strings—
They soon will answer to mirth again.

Oh! were it mine to choose the notes,
That should unto my harp belong,
    They should be gay,
    As the sky lark's lay,
With one sweet breath of the nightingale's song.

CASTLE BUILDING.

You may smile at the fanciful structures I rear,
   And say, that my castles are built but on sand;
Like bubbles, that on the blue waters appear,
   That sparkle, invite, and then sink from the hand.

When my spirit is tracing some bright and new sphere,
As light as the moment, when joy gave it birth;
   Would you stop her gay pinion, and chain her down here
To reality's region—a plodder on earth?

Tho' time, as its shadows and sorrows pass by,
  Darkens many a tint, fancy brighten'd in vain;
Their shade it will flit, like the clouds o'er the sky,
  And the picture be colour'd as gaily again.

Unlike the Pactolus, which glisten'd of old,
  But whose waves have exhausted their own brilliant store;
The fountain of hope is still sparkling with gold,
  And often applied to, but proffers the more.

FABLE.

[Imitated from the French of La Motte.]

Four souls, that on earth had just yielded their breath,
Were by Mercury led to the regions of death:
A father, who left wife and children behind,
A hero, a poet, their honours resign'd;
A maiden, to whom the cold death-warrant came
At the critical moment of changing her name.

Oh, love ! cried the fair, I less mourn for my doom,
Than for the dear youth who now weeps o'er my tomb ;
For soon will his ashes, commingled with mine,
Seal vows, so oft plighted, at constancy's shrine.
Alas ! quoth the sire, at this moment I see
My wife and my children lamenting for me ;
The thought of their sorrow's despair to my soul;
May heaven, in pity, their anguish console !
And what is their grief, pray ?—the hero replied ;
What are you ?—a poor pitiful ghost by my side.
From the north frozen desert, to Africa's sands,
Unrivall'd my name crown'd with victory stands.
Who is there on earth, whose presumption dares claim
A glory like mine, in the annals of fame ?
I dare ! said the poet ; oh ! ever will bloom,
The justly gain'd laurels that twine round my tomb :

The trophies I've won are more durable far,
Than the splendour which glitters round victory's
    car;
Long ages to come, will remember my strain;
Oh! when will a harp, like to mine, wake again!
Indeed, cried the god, I half grieve to dispel
Illusions, which now seem to please you so well;
But know, my fair maiden, your well belov'd
    youth
Has wedded another,—great proof of his truth:
And, father, instead of regretting your fate,
Your children, at law squabble for your estate;
Your wife seems to think you no very great loss,
For, as you grew old, you grew stingy and cross.
And, general, already your laurels decay—
Fresh wreaths are adorning the chief of the day:
And you, my fine poet, who thought that the earth
To another such minstrel could never give birth,

Already your works are all thrown on the shelf,
And their author condemn'd as an ignorant elf.—
Yes; look thro' the world, and this truth you will
    find—
That, once out of sight, you are soon out of mind.

SKETCH OF SCENERY.

It was a little glen, which, like a thing
Cherish'd in secret, as a treasure hid
From all the world, lay bosom'd in those heights;
'Twas such a spot, as in all ages men
Have sacred held: the Greek had said, it was
Some fabled wood-nymph's favourite dwelling
    place;
And former minstrels of our isle had deem'd,
The fairies chose it for their moonlight haunt:
Fed by a mountain rill, which softly fell—

Quiet, like patient tears, a fountain rose.
In spring, the violet and primrose breathed
Their sighs upon the banks; for tho' the flowers
Had pass'd away, the green leaves spread around,
'Mid the soft turf;—but tho' the scented race
Of April blooms were gone, yet there were still
Bright odourous blossoms: there the pale pink
      heath
Grew in its delicate beauty; and the blue
Of the fair harebell seem'd as it had caught
Its azure from the wave. You might not gaze
At distance round, for lofty trees uprose,
And rocky summits clos'd it in. The noon
Had here no power; it was most sweet to lean,
In the hot summer hours, upon that bank,
And watch the sun beams o'er the waters play,
Just where they left the hill side and came down,
In a light diamond shower, silently,
Yourself in shade the while; for o'er that rill

An ancient beech spread its deep canopy:
Some one had planted there a pale white rose;
And the wild ones sweetly blush'd beside, and twin'd
Around the lovely stranger, as they would
Give it kind welcome. Never more my steps
Will wander in thy solitude, lone glen!
I shall not list again the serenade
The wood lark pours unto the eve; or wish,
When that I saw a green leaf float along
Upon the sunny waters of thy stream,
That such might be the fate of those I lov'd—
A bright untroubled course; and when the gale,
Too rudely breathing, whirl'd the leaf away,
Bethink me of how very vain my wish.
It is not grief, to say farewell to thee,
Valley of beauty! even in thy shades
I felt as exiles feel, when far from those
With whom their heart's love dwells: I have oft
    look'd

Upon the clouds, and envied them the wind
That bore them on.   All lovely as thou art,
'Tis joy to think, that when to-morrow's sun
Shall sink amid those woods, my anxious eye
Will gaze on scenes most precious to my soul,
That have so long been memory's resting place,
Where every hope of happiness is shrin'd.

LINES TO ——

No, no! thou hast broken the spell that entwin'd me—
   The heart thou hast slighted, beats for thee no more;
Once, fondly and truly this bosom inshrin'd thee;
   But now that vain dream of a moment is o'er.

I lov'd thee with all young love's wild devotion,
   While thou wert as fickle as yon changing sea;
But think not, returning, like calm to that ocean,
   The wanderer will ever be welcome to me.

Oh! deem not again love's sweet lamp may be
    lighted—
You may never relink the once-severed chain;
When once thou hadst broken the vows that were
    plighted,
My soul was too proud to receive them again.

LINES

ADDRESSED TO MISS BISSET.

CAME it not like enchantment on the soul,
Chaining the very life pulse with delight!
Each feeling lost in one delicious dream,
All hush'd in that deep harmony. If yet
This earth can boast a trace of Paradise,
One relic of its former state, 'tis that
Which yet survives in music's hallow'd sigh.
If ever that sweet spirit, whose rich breath,

Is on the evening gale which murmurs by,
Fraught with the nightingale and wood lark's song,
Or wafting from the moonlight waves soft notes
Of airy melody from the wind wak'd shells
In the blue waters of the sea, ere gave
His power, his magic power, to human hand,
He gifted thee! Thine every witching tone,
In which the soul of music lives; light sounds,
Sweet as a lover's serenade, or wild
As minstrelsy that thrills a minstrel's dream,
Or the deep swell of inspiration's glow—
All are thine own, Cecilia of our isle!

FRAGMENT.

I saw her amid pleasure's gayest haunts—
Her black hair bound with roses, which grew pale
By the vermilion of the cheek's rich dye;
And when she mov'd, those ebon tresses wav'd
Upon the air, as love's wing had just past
And fann'd them: such a lip of sweets and smiles
Young Hebe wore, when treading 'mid the stars,
Herself a fairer one, she held the cup
Of sparkling nectar. She was, 'mid the gay,
The gayest of the throng; in her dark eye,

Where soul and softness mingled, there was mirth,
Gleaming like light from the long shadowy lash,
Which on it hung like night—but such a night
As when the moon look'd forth in loveliness.
She mov'd amid the dance, light as the wind,
At which the tremulous aspen scarcely bends.
Beautiful girl ! ah, who that saw thee there—
Joy in thy steps, and smiles upon thy brow,
Thy cheek so warm with life and gaiety—
Could deem those smiles, those blushes were thy
    last !
Pass but a little moment, and those eyes
Would close in endless sleep ! that even now
The hand of death is on thee !——
There is the wreath she wore; the roses yet
Retain a breath of sweetness ; but the brow
Round which they twin'd, is low in the cold grave !

LINES.

She kneels by the grave where her lover sleeps;
   With a cypress and rose she has crown'd it;
And there her lonely vigil keeps,
   While the moonlight beams surround it.

Her hair is loose to the chill night gale;
   No more with spring flowers she'll braid it:
Her dark eye is dim, her cheek is pale—
   Sorrow can swiftly fade it.

She has knelt by that grave for many a day—
  Morn and even still found her beside it:
Soon will that mourner be past away—
  Her grief, the cold grave will hide it.

Her spring of youth was fair for awhile,
  And then the dark cloud came o'er it;
When once the blight checks the rose's smile,
  Where is the spell to restore it?

THE STORM.

There was a vessel combating the waves,
Like one who struggles with adversity :
The sea has wash'd her decks, and the wet sails
Hang droopingly ; by the blue lightning's flash—
Light horrible and strange—there might be seen
All shapes of wild despair ; the clasped hands,
Rais'd in scarce-conscious prayer, the cold white lip,
The stern fix'd brow, which braves the death that yet

The fainting pulses tremble at ; **and** sounds
Of sobs suppress'd, and mutter'd words, were heard,
When the winds sank in low and solemn wail—
A breathing space of terror, but to rouse
More fearfully. That tempest had swept o'er
The awaken'd deep so suddenly, it seem'd
As some unholy spell had call'd it forth—
Summon'd, unthought of, from its secret home.
Lost in the fair blue sky, where scarce a cloud
Was seen, save those that threw their rosy wreaths
Upon the west, to hail the approaching sun,
Like flowers strewn upon the conqueror's way.
The ocean hush'd in beautiful repose,
Seem'd fitting mirror for the pale young moon,
And the soft light of the sweet evening star.
Sailing in majesty and loveliness,
The vessel cut the waters, which did seem
To pay her homage, as unto their queen ;
And far in the horizon was a speck,

Scarce visible, but watch'd as anxiously
As would a mother watch the first faint tinge
Of health revisiting her child's wan cheek,
Where every thought and hope had long time
    clung—
Light of the voyage drear—their native shore.
A sound breaks the still silence, and a cloud
Is gathering on the air : that sound is not
The tumult of the storm ; and the dark roll
Of yon black volume, rising streak'd with fire,
Is not the tempest's dwelling ;—'tis the breath,
The fiery breath of war ; and man has dar'd
Profane the quiet of an hour like this !
Battle ! destruction !—does the world contain
One spot, whereon your baneful taint is not ?—
A thicker darkness gathers ; 'tis not now
Alone the dense smoke curling ; hark, yon roll !
Echoing the cannon, as in mockery.
The winds have burst their slumber, and are risen,

Like waken'd giants, wrathful at their rest.
The foes are sunder'd; there is many a cheek,
Late warm with pride of battle, pale and cold.
Came not the storm upon their warfare like
A sign, a fearful warning?—on it swept;
Foam crested the dark billows as they dash'd,
Like armed warriors rushing to the field
Upon the shore; and gleaming flashes rose,
As when the clashing weapons meet in war.
And still against the moveless rock, the sea
Led on her armies; and the howling winds
Pour'd their war-song in murmurs, fierce and loud,
As they did triumph in the desolate power
That urg'd them now. There was just light enough
To show the black clouds hung upon the sky,
Like ministers of vengeance; and the swell
Of the pil'd waters—that most fearful sight
Of human creatures perishing, with scarce
One moment's warning ere their doom is seal'd.

145

The lightnings rush'd, and that tost ship is seen
Rais'd on the mountain waves—another flash!
There are the angry billows—but no trace
Of living thing is seen.

TO SIR JOHN DOYLE, Bart.

My heart has beat high at the heroes of old,
 As they live in those annals of fame,
Where the deeds of their glory are glowingly told,
 When history has hallow'd their name.
It was pride, as I thought on those sunbeams of yore,
 Like vessels of light on oblivion's dark seas,
To pass o'er those ages, and think my own shore
 Had many, whose names would shine brightly as these.

Who has not proudly dwelt on those memories of light,
And felt them, like something that glorified earth?
Who has not exclaim'd, with a burst of delight—
'Tis my own native land which has given them birth!
Yes, warrior! 'tis only high spirits like thine,
That teach man the generous path he may tread;
The steps of the mighty are nature's best shrine,
Where the hopes of the young and aspiring are fed.
Yes, warrior! when young hearts shall pant for the praise,
Such praise as the praise of the valiant will be,
He will think of the splendour that brighten'd thy days;—
He will think of that splendour, and imitate thee.

Hail, honour and pride of the Emerald Isle!
　How envied the mead that will ever be thine !
The laurel of fame, and humanity's smile,
　To grace thee, shall always together combine.
The soldier, worn down by war's strife and turmoil,
　No longer's left cheerless and friendless to roam;
For the rest of his age may be grateful to Doyle,
　For the sweets of his hearth, and the peace of his home.

FRAGMENT.*

Is not this grove
A scene of pensive loveliness? The gleam
Of Dian's gentle ray falls o'er the trees,
And piercing thro' the gloom, seems like the smile
That pity gives to cheer the brow of grief.
The turf has caught a silvery hue of light,
Broken by shadows, where the branching oak
Rears its dark shade, or where the aspen waves
Its trembling leaves; the breeze is murmuring by,
Fraught with sweet sighs of flowers, and the song

* This is the only Poem in the volume previously published: it appeared in the Literary Gazette.

Of sorrow, that the nightingale pours forth,
Like the soft dirge of love.——
     There is oft told
A melancholy record of this grove—
It was time once the haunt of young affection;
And now seems hallow'd by the tender vows
That erst were breathed here. Sad is the tale
That tells of blighted feelings—hopes destroyed;
But love is like the rose, so many ills
Assail it in the bud—the canker worm,
The frost of winter, and the summer storm,
All blow it down; rarely the blossom comes
To full maturity. But there is nought
Sinks with so chill a breath as faithlessness—
As she could tell, whose loveliness yet lives
In village legends. Often at this hour
Of lonely beauty, would she list the tale
Of tenderness, and hearken to the vows
Of one, more dear than life unto her soul.

He twin'd him round a heart, which beat with all
The deep devotedness of early love;
Then left her, careless of the passion which
He had awakened into wretchedness.
The blight, which wither'd all the blossoms love
Had fondly cherish'd, wither'd too the heart
Which gave them birth; her sorrow had no voice,
Save in her faded beauty, for she look'd
A melancholy broken-hearted girl:
She was so chang'd, the soft carnation cloud,
Once mantling o'er her cheek, like those which eve
Hangs o'er the twilight of a summer sky,
Was faded into paleness, broken by
Bright burning blushes—torches of the tomb.
There was such sadness even in her smiles,
And such a look of utter hopelessness
Dwelt in her soft blue eyes, a form so frail,
So delicate, scarce like a thing of earth :—
'Twas sad to gaze upon a brow so fair,

And see it trac'd with such a tale of woe:
To think that one so young and beautiful,
Was wasting to the grave !
     Within yon bower
Of honey-suckle, and the snowy wealth
The mountain ash puts forth to welcome spring,
Her form was found, reclin'd upon a bank ;
Where nature's sweet unnurtur'd children bloom'd:
One white arm lay beneath her drooping head,
While her bright tresses twin'd their sunny wreath
Around the polish'd ivory ; there was not
A tinge of colour mantling o'er her face ;
'Twas like to marble, where the sculptor's skill
Has trac'd each charm of beauty, save the blush.
Serenity so sweet sat on her brow ;
So soft a smile yet hover'd on her lips ;
At first they thought 'twas sleep—and sleep it was,
The cold long rest of death.——
There is one grave, o'er which the cypress bends,

ADDRESSED TO ——

THE bee, when varying flowers are nigh,
   On many a sweet will careless dwell;
Just sips their dew, and then will fly
   Again to its own cherish'd cell.
Thus, tho' my heart by fancy led,
   A wanderer for awhile may be;
Yet, soon returning whence it fled,
   Comes but more fondly back to thee.

W. Pople, Printer, 67, Chancery Lane.

Like a devoted mourner; there are laid
The lost remains of one, once beautiful
Belov'd, and young. Upon her marble urn
Some hand affectionate has simply carv'd
A touching emblem of her early fate—
A lilly, sever'd from its stem, and wither'd,
Yet lovely in decay.

INDEXES

Index of Titles

Absence ("And all the fix'd delights of house and home"), 75
Absence ("Oh! never can we feel how dear"), 110
Addressed to ——, 154
Answer, 105
Answer to ——, 121
Castle Building, 123
Corinna, 97
Curtius, 77
Dirge, 107
Fable, 125
Farewell, The, 69
Fate of Adelaide, The, Canto I., 1
——, Canto II., 33
Fragment ("I saw her amid pleasure's gayest haunts–"), 137
Fragment ("Is not this grove"), 149
Fragment ("It is not spring, but still the new-come year"), 91
Fragment ("Love thee! yes, yes! the storms that rend aside"), 73
Lines ("She kneels by the grave where her lover sleeps"), 139
Lines Addressed to Colonel H——, on his return from Waterloo, 101
Lines Addressed to Miss Bisset, 135
Lines on ——, 88
Lines to —— ("No, no! thou hast broken the spell that entwin'd me–"), 133
Lines to —— ("Think of me, and I'll tell thee when"), 71
Love's Choice, 116
Love's Parting Wreath, 103
Lover's Dream, A, 113
Miscellaneous Poems, 67
Phoenix and the Dove, The, 115
Portrait, 93
Sketch of a Painting of Santa Malvidera, 81
Sketch of Scenery, 129
Sleeping Child, 99
Sonnet ("Green willow! over whom the perilous blast"), 83
Sonnet ("I envy not the traveller's delight"), 109

INDEX OF TITLES

Sonnet ("It is not in the day of revelry"), 84
Stanzas ("I do not weep that thou art laid"), 85
Stanzas, Adapted to Music by ———, 119
Star, The, 117
Storm, The, 141
To ———, 95
To Sir John Doyle, Bart., 146
Village of the Lepers, The, 86

Index of First Lines

Came it not like enchantment on the soul, 135
Farewell! companion of my solitude! 69
Four souls, that on earth had just yielded their breath, 125
Green willow! over whom the perilous blast, 83
How innocent, how beautiful thy sleep! 99
I do not weep that thou art laid, 85
I envy not the traveller's delight, 109
I gaz'd admiringly upon his face, 93
I give thee, love, a blooming braid, 103
I saw her amid pleasure's gayest haunts–, 137
I saw thy cheek when 'twas fresh as spring, 88
I will not say, I fear your absent one, 75
Is not this grove/ . . ., 149
It is not in the day of revelry, 84
It is not spring, but still the new-come year, 91
It was a dream, as bright as e'er, 113
It was a little glen, which, like a thing, 129
Love thee! yes, yes! the storms that rend aside, 73
My heart has beat high at the heroes of old, 146
My heart is as light as the gossamer veil, 119
My wings are bright with the rainbow's dyes, 115
No, no! thou hast broken the spell that entwin'd me–, 133
Oh, calm be thy slumbers, 107
Oh! never can we feel how dear, 110
Oh! say not, that I love not nature's face, 95
Oh! would I might share thy wild car, 117
Once more my harp awakens; once again, 33
Romantic Switzerland! thy scenes are traced, 1
She kneels by the grave where her lover sleeps, 139
She knelt upon the rock; her graceful arms, 81
She stood alone; but on her every eye, 97
The bee, when varying flowers are nigh, 154
The wreath you gave me, love, is dead, 105
There is a multitude, in number like, 77
There was a curse upon the unhappy race, 86

INDEX OF FIRST LINES

There was a vessel combating the waves, 141
Think of me, and I'll tell thee when, 71
Too long the daring power of love, 116
Twine not the cypress round my harp, 121
Who envies not the glory of the brave! 101
You may smile at the fanciful structures I rear, 123